HEAL YOUR
WAY FORWARD

HEAL YOUR WAY FORWARD

THE CO-CONSPIRATOR'S GUIDE TO AN ANTIRACIST FUTURE

....

MYISHA T HILL

Row House Publishing recognizes that the power of justice-centered storytelling isn't a phenomenon; it is essential for progress. We believe in equity and activism, and that books—and the culture around them—have the potential to transform the universal conversation around what it means to be human.

Part of honoring that conversation is protecting the intellectual property of authors. Reproducing any portion of this book (except for the use of short quotations for review purposes) without the expressed written permission of the copyright owner(s) is strictly prohibited. Submit all requests for usage to rights@rowhousepublishing.com.

Thank you for being an important part of the conversation and holding sacred the critical work of our authors.

Library of Congress Cataloging-in-Publication Data Available Upon Request
ISBN 978-1-955905-02-2 (HC)
ISBN 978-1-955905-08-4 (eBook)
Printed in the United States
Distributed by Simon & Schuster

Book design by Pauline Neuwirth, Neuwirth & Associates, Inc.

First edition
10 9 8 7 6 5 4 3 2

I dedicate this living work to myself as a radical act of self-love. I have finally come home to myself. To anyone whom I have caused harm while trying to find myself as a neurodivergent Black woman in an imperialist capitalist white supremacist ableist world. To all embodying the practice of being whole and human. In the essence of Ubuntu, I am because you are.

"I want my work to be about healing."

—bell hooks

On December 15, 2021, I was shaken by the death of bell hooks, along with the rest of the world. I spent a couple of days on a roller coaster of grief, cycling through emotions. I felt sorry for not visiting bell hooks at Berea College. Shame and blame riddled me as I questioned if I'd adequately credited the great elder-now-ancestor for inspiring so much of my work. And so now, I ponder at this moment: Where do I go from here? How do I accept this loss and grow from it?

First, remember. This work is about healing. This work should be rooted in love, and love is, in fact, the work. bell hooks said, "Right now, there is such a profound collective cultural awareness that we need to practice love if we are to heal ourselves and the planet. The task awaiting us is to move from awareness to action. The practice of love requires that we make time, that we embrace change."

bell hooks was calling us into the practice of love.

I want to thank her for inspiring me to move into a love ethic. For calling me into something bigger than myself. For teaching me that, as a Black woman, my words are poignant and powerful and that writing can be a healing journey. Like bell hooks, I want to be remembered not for who I am but for the work I've done in the world. May the words of this book bring forth divinely inspired transformation, restoration, and justice.

bell hooks, I thank you for being. Rest well, ancestor.

—myisha t hill

CONTENTS

FOREWORD

BY AYCEE BROWN

On May 25, 2020, a video was uploaded on social media. Another unarmed Black man was killed in broad daylight at the hands of cops. But this time was even more traumatic, as George Floyd called out for his mother while a cop had his entire body weight kneeling on his neck, cutting off his circulation. It went viral, and Black and Brown people experienced yet another trauma. I tried not to watch the video but I did. We all tried not to watch it but we did. Now that day is forever imprinted on our minds.

As a young Black girl, I'd seen videos on the news of Rodney King getting beaten by the police, and later in life, I'd seen Eric Garner shout the words "I can't breathe" while being put in a chokehold as he was getting arrested. But George Floyd was different. The image of him lying on the ground not resisting was different. What stood out the most was the look on Derek Chauvin's face. I was familiar with it—the look of superiority. He looked into the camera and didn't care. Even as the cameras recorded him, there was no fear. It immediately brought tears to my eyes as I flashed back to moments of getting pulled over by the cops and calling a friend or my parents just so they could listen in, just in case anything happened to me. Even though I'd done nothing wrong or maybe turned a corner too fast or went through a yellow light right before it turned red.

When Black people get murdered at the hands of the police, we don't think it's a random case. Our first instinct as Black people is always *that could've been me*. It could've been our fathers, mothers, cousins, uncles, aunts, and friends. We don't have the luxury to be exempt from death by the police. We have a long history in this country with it. It's in our DNA, and no one should have to hold that much trauma in their body, currently or generationally.

But as a Black woman in America, my body holds many traumatic memories, including those that I've seen and those that have been passed down to me. All Black and Brown people do. The sudden wake-up call that white America experienced in the next few days after the murder of George Floyd threw me and others off guard. I, as well as many other content creators, started speaking out about the disparities in our niches. From calling out big brands to influencers, it was our time to tell the truth of what was really happening behind the scenes. As a Black woman in the spirituality and self-help space, I was angry and went on social media and talked about my own gripes and frustration about not being seen in that sphere. And then I started receiving DMs from people in my industry who hadn't reached out before, even people whom I'd invited on my podcast and never responded. It felt as if they wanted to right years of wrongs with a direct message. It was almost as though for the last two hundred years they saw nothing wrong with what was happening in the world and now they needed to come together and support us. That was the most heartbreaking part of this traumatic event—the performances of non–people of color, from corporations to influencers, the black square, the social media break for a week to "shine" a light on Black and Brown creators. I remember a creator saying make sure you all keep that same energy when the dust settles. And the dust has settled and we are back to normal. Well, non–people of color are, but the rest of us still live in this world every day with harsh realities that, yes, we've made progress, but we still have so far to go.

A few years before this tragedy, Myisha told me she was going to put all her energy into Check Your Privilege because she was passionate about educating non–people of color about the disparities in communities, government, religion, and the workplace. She was passionate and yet she kept hitting brick walls. I remember late-night phone calls filled with tears about what she was trying to do and how no one was hearing her. At times, she questioned what was the point. I would encourage her that her voice needed to be heard. Myisha was working in a religious space and would talk about how racism is so strong in Christianity and it was making her sick. Her mental health was being jeopardized daily and it was hard for her most days. Her experiences at her job fueled her passion in doing this work. She was living what she was talking about. I felt her pain and I knew what it was like to have to keep your mouth closed in order to survive at a job that clearly doesn't have your best interest at heart. Is it unfair that when things are blatantly racist at work, you feel your livelihood is on the line? Being quiet doesn't fix the problem, but speaking up is so risky. And that's a reality for many Black and Brown folx. Black and Brown folx in the workplace have had to silence ourselves in spaces that are predominantly white so we wouldn't seem like troublemakers. I would tell her to keep fighting, keep educating. She did. And thank goodness she did.

Myisha kept fighting for awareness around these issues, and she finally began to receive it. And yet there is still so much work to be done. There are still so many eyes that haven't been opened. But how do we do this work without breaking our backs educating white people? How do we make change without becoming the morality police? I truly don't know. But I do know that it starts with inclusion: including more Black and Brown folx in spaces that are predominantly white, such as conferences, corporate boards, educational boards, and politics. We need to be seen in these spaces because our voices matter. But our counterparts have to be willing to go against the grain and include us. They have to invite us in.

It's time for healing, but what most white people need to know is that there is no prize for healing and change. Many speak of inclusion, but are you yourself ready to be inclusive? Because in order to do this work, there must be radical transparency. There must be a willingness to make real change that involves action. Is this possible? Yes, but only for those who are ready. Ready to leave behind the old constructs that don't benefit Black and Brown people. For this, Myisha has the answers. She has the answers to help the non-performance of change. Because an anti-racist future looks like non-POC people extending a helping hand and making their resources available to us. It includes being open to hearing about the disparities without being defensive. It means non-POC people healing their own biases about Black and Brown folx and choosing to do better and not just talking about it. Myisha is working toward helping us all heal and have an understanding of what that looks like for both sides. She's educating, informing, and providing tools for change. She's shining a light on systematic racism. It's going to take time, just like anything, but it can be done. And it's going to take a collective effort. That starts with you reading this book. It starts with you having uncomfortable conversations. It starts with you calling out the people around you because you know better, so it's your responsibility to do better. This is your moment to rewrite history and be a change agent in this lifetime. Don't miss your opportunity to do so.

HEAL YOUR
WAY FORWARD

INTRODUCTION

"Not everything that is faced can be changed, but
nothing can be changed until it is faced."
—James Baldwin

I am Black and beautiful. Like you, my life has been full of nuance and trauma, and as an ode to Langston Hughes's "Mother to Son," we can say that "My life isn't no crystal stair." In fact, according to some, I have been a societal misfit. But I believe our stories are sacred, and it is through our individual and collective stories that we learn more about ourselves and the greater collective. Story captures us and teaches us insights for the future. Storytelling connects us and heals us forward. In my ancestral lineage, we used oral storytelling so that we could learn from the mistakes of the past. More than fourteen generations ago, my ancestors, members of the Akan tribe in Ghana, left through their door of no return. The stories that unfolded from there not only form the basis of my personal history but of the collective history of the culture in which I, and likely you, grew up.

I was born in Cook County hospital on the south side of Chicago. My parents were never married, and I was raised by my momma, grandmother, and the maternal side of the family. On my father's side, my older brothers and my grandmother maintained connection with me throughout childhood. I was loved, nurtured, and nourished via matriarchy and Western Christianity, all of which made me feel I didn't belong in this world. According to white culture, I've always been seen as inadequate, inferior, and a failure. But I wasn't raised to believe the myth of white supremacy, or anti-Blackness. In fact, I was raised to appreciate my heritage, serve my community, and know my place as a Black woman in the world, which meant don't rock the boat, stir up trouble, or speak too loudly.

I grew up socially withdrawn, but I didn't know I had a choice. I was told "not to speak" and to only "be seen," so what else are you supposed to do? My mom would say I was selectively mute because as a child I would just point to things and grunt. The thing is I could hear words in my head and yet nothing would come out. It wouldn't be until I fought for my son's autism diagnosis that I recognized that I was an undiagnosed autistic child. With two of my children having high-functioning autism and one with ADHD, it doesn't surprise me that I would be seemingly disabled. If you know me and my work, you may be a bit in shock. Because the woman you see speaking out against oppression didn't speak for years, socialized to believe her voice didn't matter.

It wouldn't be until I was in fifth grade living in California when my best friend, Janine Lee, became the spark for me to find my voice. We moved a lot when I was younger, spending four years in Berkeley and then four years in Chicago to take care of my grandma. In Chicago, my mother was a plus-size fashion model and put me in modeling and charm school for three years.

I was always in awe of how she could walk a runway, transforming into a woman who was so full of life. My mother spent her time working, modeling, and enjoying her youth as much as she could. She had a strong work ethic that I didn't understand. Instead, I felt abandoned by her absence. But it was this same work ethic that taught me how to hustle, believing that as long as I overworked, life would be okay. While my mother was gone, my grandmother took care of me, which meant I spent a lot of time in church, volunteering, visiting elders, or going to nursing homes all in the name of service and Jesus. My grandmother was an awesome woman, almost like a mother to me. I learned from her how to serve from my heart, give to the community, love all people, and forgive those who hurt you, among several other Christian lessons. What I realized was that socialized Christianity is what created a pattern for me to be taken advantage of and not have the boundaries to say no.

In 1992, we relocated to California. My momma didn't want me to become a statistic in Chicago, having babies by thirteen like a lot of the young girls around us. So, at the start of fifth grade, I moved in with my aunt in Oakland, in the Temescal neighborhood. Oakland was beautiful and filled with the rich culture of my people (East Fourteenth and Durant Square reminded me of Bronzeville on the south side of Chicago). I loved Oakland and it broke my heart when I learned that we would soon be leaving for Concord, California, where my mom thought we would find a better life. Even at the time, moving to Concord didn't seem like a good idea to me, but as I got older, I realized it was where I learned to uphold whiteness over my own Black identity. It would become my white culture training 101.

Leaving Oakland for Concord was like something you'd see in a movie: Leave the bustle of the city, hit the highway, drive through the affluent Oakland Hills and into the Caldecott Tunnel. On the other side of the tunnel, you're met with a whole new world. Grassy knolls and clean highways were the path to the 'burbs and toward Mount Diablo. You could tell this community was full of folx who escaped the cities when redlining was no longer an option. Concord was a historically upper-class white community with a history steeped in the KKK and segregation. In fact, you knew when you should and shouldn't go outside in Concord. The buses ran every hour and we had to walk with a shopping cart to get to the nearest grocery store.

Growing up in Concord was fascinating. Despite its whiteness, it was the place where I learned to speak and have a voice. Though most of the teachers were very biased toward white folx and many of the gifted students where predominantly male and white, most of my friends were multiethnic, and we took pride in being "diverse" and not seeing color. When my mom, brother, and I would go back to Oakland, my peers would tell me that I talked and thought white. I never paid attention to it though because I thought it was a badge of honor to live in a "better place" and have friends of all races. Most of the white kids were cool until we got to middle school, and that's where the bullying began. During that time, I would often get bullied by the white boys at school who found joy in calling me Wanda from *In Living Color* or Sheneneh Jenkins from *Martin*.

I wasn't sure what to do with the cruel treatment, so my mom and grandma got me into cheerleading. We couldn't really afford it, so they would fundraise from their friends to pay for my cheerleading things. I think my grandmother even began ironing T-shirts as a side hustle to help with this and other bills around the house. A lot of the funding also came from my grandmother's friends from church. Thus began my deep dive into white Christianity. I didn't fit in, and no one looked liked me. However, I will never forget Courtney and Vanessa, who always made space and time to talk to me. Courtney was one of my few "close" youth group members, though I wouldn't see her again until October 2019 at a speaking engagement. But I could have conversations with Courtney and Vanessa even outside of the church, talking pop culture, dreams of growing up, and what faith really meant.

I was also one of the first folx to know about one of my friends struggling with their identity. Because story is sacred, I want to respect her trust in me. I will say that those two friendships normalized standing out and supporting each other in community, even if the community was an all-white youth group. My mom believed the youth group was "an access pass," sending me on ski trips, backpacking, camping, and "mission" trips all in the name of a white liberal Jesus. Each summer we'd volunteer at Opportunity Camp in the Santa Cruz Mountains, a Christian camp for kids from lower-income communities in Contra Costa County, California. But I saw myself as different from the Black youth we served because I was the volunteer; I wasn't "like them." Now I see how that sense of othering is what leads to economic and class privilege among the Black community.

For eight years, I was on the cheerleading team and in the youth group. But at the age of fourteen, I was sexually traumatized by a high school senior. I didn't tell my mother until Tamara Burke's #MeToo movement went viral. I was too afraid to share my truth because at the time of the incident, I was with the daughter of the CEO at the big company where my mother worked. Secrets were what kept me in a cycle of pain and trauma from which I would spend most of my life running.

Upon graduation, I wanted to pursue Black livelihood, moving back to Chicago to take care of my grandpa, find work, and go to school. In my head, I left to be famous. But that didn't work out, as I found out he lived with a mood disorder, and at eighteen, I was not equipped to deal with it. Instead, I decided to move to Madison, Wisconsin, to live with my paternal side of the family. The years between eighteen and twenty-two were some of the most traumatic and hardest years of my life. I will not divulge details of that experience, but I will say trauma and boundary violations would reshape my identity as a Black woman. In those years, I had three miscarriages but found hope as a cashier at Home Depot where I met my God family who cared for and nurtured me back to my healing.

At the age of twenty-two, my mom decided to move to the Midwest with my little brother. In Madison, I got myself into trouble and eventually had to move to the cornfields of DeKalb, Illinois. It was there I found out I was pregnant. During my pregnancy, I went back to school. Not knowing the scam of student loans, I spent years living on Section 8 and student loans as I worked to get a degree and have a better life for me and my son. When my son was two and a half, I got into plus-size fashion and felt like I was on top of the world. I created X'Change Modeling to help plus-size women around the world gain confidence. It was an adventure of a lifetime, but that all changed when I found out I was pregnant again. Around that time, my eldest son was diagnosed with sensory processing disorder. Prior to his diagnosis, I would tell doctors something wasn't right with him. He would thrash and have night terrors and display seizure-like behavior. In fact, when he was two weeks old, his eyes rolled back in his head, and he stopped breathing in his sleep. He was given a spinal tap at the hospital and diagnosed with sleep apnea. He was put on a breathing machine for six months. It was a relief to finally have one of many diagnoses to help him get the tools he needed in the school system.

When I found out I was pregnant with my second child, I felt like a failure. Pre-partum depression sunk in, and I didn't want to do anything, but I kept on with my modeling and plus-size pageantry. When Melech was born, I had a great support system and I ended up transferring to a four-year university. All seemed well, but then I became pregnant again. This time I had to withdraw from school, quit fashion, and could no longer live on my own. Instead, I had to temporarily move back home with my mother. Pre-partum depression, and suicidal ideation, became the norm. My mom didn't know what to do; there would be days I would be up and days I'd be down. I struggled with the idea that I would once again be a single mom on welfare. I considered myself a menace to society, a welfare queen. The stigma of baby daddies and welfare checks challenged my ability to see that temporary help as okay.

When my son Micah was seven, my son Melech was twenty-two months, and my daughter Naima was twelve days old, I lost my will to live. I was ashamed and my self-esteem was shot. I thought, *Who's going to love me now?* Things had become so dark in my life that I couldn't see a way out.

Imagine yourself walking in a dark, sealed tunnel and all you can do is go from one end to the other. There's no air. And you feel like the life is being sucked out of you. That is what my battle with suicide felt like. There was no life. But eventually, there was a glimmer. Her name was Jeanette. I called Jeanette and told her, I *can't live anymore. Life is too hard; I don't want to do this anymore.* She called my mom and then stayed on the phone until my mom arrived. It felt like it was all moving so fast.

The next thing I knew I was in the emergency room, and then I was moved to a secluded section with glass and white walls and no TV and I was like, *Okay. Now, I'm crazy.* I thought Black people didn't go crazy. That's a white people thing, you know? I believed the good Lord was supposed to un-crazy me. Before I knew it, they told me, "We're going to take you to a mental health institution." Okay. Black folx don't do mental hospitals either.

But I went. The ambulance arrived to transport me to a hospital thirty-five minutes away from my mother who took on my three kids, including my newborn daughter. On the way to the ambulance, I'll never forget my mother's face and the pain in her eyes. As she looked at the daughter, now a grown woman with three young children of her own, her face was filled with questions: *Are we gonna get through this? Will her children recover? Hell, will she recover? Do I have to, as a former single mother, become a single mother again to three young children?*

I remembered speeding to this "hospital." And then we stopped. We went inside. It was quiet. Have you seen *Girl, Interrupted*, that movie with Angelina Jolie? Like with the doors? That's a real thing, I was like, *All right, how many other white folx went through this?* So, they took me off the stretcher and put me in a wheelchair. And then a lady was like, "We need you to voluntarily sign yourself in." What? I was so confused but I signed in.

And then they said, "Here's some anxiety medication. It's going to help you take the edge off." I'm Black; I don't take medication. The only medication that Black and Brown people take is for high cholesterol and diabetes.

The next morning, I woke up in the hospital. My roommate was this funky old white lady, about sixty-five with four grandkids. This was in Dekalb, Illinois, so all she talked about was the country and the grandkids and her farm and her husband and I was like, *Okay, cool.* And then she told me, "I've been in and out of this place for the last fifteen years." And I was like, *Ah hell no, that ain't gonna be me. Not today, Satan.*

It was in that moment that I was like, *Okay, I must be here for a reason.* I walked into the lobby, and guess what the first thing I saw was? It was a Bible. And the one thing I knew growing up in the church and being a strong-willed Black woman was that that Bible meant that there was a higher calling for my life and this experience was going to be used to bless somebody. Real talk. And I live that truth to this day. Seeing that Bible was God, the universe, Buddha, whatever you believe in, offering a sign that, baby girl, I'm here for you. It's going to be all right, and you're going to help somebody.

So, the Bible became my best friend. I walked around the hospital with that Bible and a journal and wrote every day. I would find scripture and ask myself, how does this scripture relate to me being in a mental health hospital? So, then my pastors came, including my Pastor Joe, who I told, "Pastor Joe, if the church had something for people of color to talk about depression and anxiety and mental illness, I wouldn't be here today." Now, I was high on medication so let's not forget that, but I remember these conversations. I continued, telling him, "One day, I'm gonna start something for people of color to talk about their mental illness." Who would have known that I was speaking Brown Sisters Speak and Iwosan Collective into existence.

And even as I sat there in that hospital, my pastor was like, "Yeah, you're right. And we're gonna support you."

I smiled, looking out onto the snowy yard outside, "You bet your good Lord you are."

When you're in the mental health hospital, you must go to what's called "Group." The people who had been there multiple times told me that the way to get out is to take medication, see the doctor, pretend that everything is okay, and attend Group.

So, I did what I was told, telling everyone I was doing great, and biding my time until they gave me my diagnosis and sent me home. Before I met with the psychiatrist, I talked to my Uncle Brian, who at the time had a nonprofit called Black Men Speak in Oakland, which empowered men of color to talk about their mental illness. He said, "Myisha, no matter what the diagnosis is, it's not a death sentence. It does not define your destiny. Keep on going."

The next day after I got my empowering speech from Uncle Brian, I went to see the doctor, who after listening to me, replied, "Sounds like you have postpartum depression psychosis and suicidal ideation with a plan. Oh, and you're bipolar." *Wait, what?* He decided all this after forty-five minutes and a few days in the hospital? I called my mom and was pissed. I said, "I don't know what this is, Mom. What is this?"

I asked the nurses to print out some information for me on bipolar disorder because I thought the path to healing would be fast. I could pray it away. But it wasn't going to be that easy.

My mom talked me through it, reminding me of what Uncle Brian said, "No matter what the diagnosis is, it's not a death sentence. It does not define your destiny." I was still in my head thinking this was a white people disease. And that I was going to be healed from it. And so, forty-eight hours later, I was released, but that was after a seven-day stay at a mental health institution. For weeks, it felt like everybody around me who was in church, who was in my life, was judging me because they knew I was in that hospital. I felt like they all "knew" I was crazy.

Once I was out, I spent hours googling cures, trying to juice, teaching Zumba, doing Zumba, because I knew health and wellness could be a pathway, but I wasn't quite sure how.

About three months out of the hospital, the suicidal feeling came back—that darkness, that tunnel, not being able to breathe.

I told my brother I was going to take a bottle of pills and he asked me for my address. Thirty minutes later, the sheriff showed up. He told me, "You know, I'm supposed to take your kids and send you back to the hospital. But there's something about you and I just can't do it. So, give me the pills and promise me you won't do this again."

I started to feel better again, my mom came to help out, and I began to believe I was cured, but then four months later, the depression came back. I was in bed, I couldn't get up, I couldn't eat. My mom said, "You got two choices, you gon' give me your kids and go do whatever you want with your life. Or you need to figure yourself out and tend to your kids."

I was a teacher's assistant and I said, *All right, this is my last $285. I'm gonna buy me a train ticket to California because that was the last place I was truly happy.* I called my cousins Simone and Wes and said, "Hey, this is what I'm going through and this is my action plan."

And they said, "C'mon."

Simone and Wes would be the lifeline to reset my life.

I got on a train with $5 in my pocket, real talk. A day and a half worth of snacks. And I went from Naperville, Illinois, to Emeryville, California. When I got there, seven days later, I had a full-time job. Three weeks later, my mom came with my kids, and two months later, we found our own apartment, where we've been living for eight years.

My breakdown led to my breakthrough, my greatest pain birthed my greatest awakening, and it led me toward the path I am on today.

You might be reading this unsure of the connection between this life story and the work I was called into with Check Your Privilege. Well, I believe that you can take pain and transmute it into power. Growing up Black, Christian, and a woman, I was taught that there are no throwaway people. That if you make space for others, you open yourself up for radical healing. Three and a half years ago, I had a disruption with a friend, which caused me to second-guess myself and question my own sanity. This friend happened to be a white woman whom I valued and trusted like a sister. Through therapy and reading, I recognized that this woman and I had a serious problem with codependency.

We decided to work through the conflict using restorative mediation, which showed me I was being pathologized for living with depression and anxiety. I was put into the one role I worked my whole life to escape—the downtrodden Black woman in need. I had done so much work to become a successful single mother, and then finally I realized it was me who was playing a role, the one whiteness kept trying to assign to me.

When we can move beyond the pathology of our identities, we can finally speak our truth. I can be neurodiverse and successful. I can be a single mother and beautiful and desired. I recognized that life isn't a binary choice between good and bad, righteous and corrupt, as I had learned in Church. I decided I wanted to create a space to help other people identify how their behavior impacts the mental health of BIPOC folx. Check Your Privilege was born from the idea that there are no throwaway people, and that if we make space for conflict in community, we can heal our relationship with ourselves and others. I didn't create this platform as a brand to make profit, but as a catalyst for transformation and change.

Check Your Privilege is an invitation to check our individual collusion within the interlocking systems of oppression. The systems of imperialism, white supremacy, abelism, colonialism, and patriarchy block us from being in true co-conspiratorship, instead leading us to maintain complicity in and apathy for our dominant cultural beliefs. CYP is not focused on the cultural phenomenon known as white privilege, as any one person can experience both privilege and marginalization. Privilege does not mean that you don't have hardships; it means that the hardships you have experienced have nothing to do with your privileged identities.

CYP takes an intersectional approach by looking at the nuances of race, class, gender, ability, neurodiversity, mental health, and more. It's about dropping into the shadows of our self and seeing how we are complicit within those interlocking systems of oppression. Because when we choose to heal ourselves, we are able to heal generations forward and back. The invitation is to check ourselves and how we individually and collectively harm BIPOC and ourselves in community. We'll venture into conversations to unlearn and relearn what it means to heal our way forward, challenging the status quo and learning to do better together.

This work is my soul's work. It is part of a larger calling in my life. And I continue to lead this work even as I watch my mother dying at the hands of systemic racism she experiences at the University of California, Berkley, where fake woke liberals demean her character by questioning her every move and white urgency and last-minute requests cause her to suffer from heart palpitations. I stay in this work to name the harm, to walk alongside, and to show how healing isn't linear but a lifelong process of helping community, today and into the future.

THE CO-CONSPIRATOR'S JOURNEY

"No matter where you are on your journey,
that's exactly where you need to be.
The next road is always ahead."

—Oprah Winfrey

Welcome to exactly where you need to be. If you are here, then you have been called in—called in to do the work, called in to show up in a different and more powerful way, called in to heal your way forward. But I'm here to tell you, healing is not a one-time event. It is not a linear process. Healing is lifelong work. Because the more you heal, the more the work is revealed to you and, usually, the more work we have to do. It's normal to come into this work ready to pull up our sleeves and get our hands dirty. That's why most co-conspirators move straight into performative action, rather than trusting the call of the real work—the call to trust the messy and complicated process of unlearning, relearning, being in community, and working toward the collective goal.

What is that goal? We are here to build a new way forward that centers the leadership, life, and journeys of Black, Brown,

Indigenous, South East Asian, Asian American, Pacific Islander, and other marginalized persons of color. I believe that as children we are born into the world faultless, knowing nothing of the world or its expectations, but over time we are shaped and conditioned by whatever world is around us. For those of us with adverse childhood experiences, we grow up as wounded healers, looking for guidance to move forward. We search for ourselves in people, places, and things. From childhood, we have been socialized to seek happiness outside of ourselves, rather than experience happiness as an extension of who we are. It isn't until we make the conscious choice to heal that we move away from the idea that a system or series of rules sets the standards for what liberation means for us. When we choose to heal, we recognize the journey as a life calling, and when we heal ourselves, we help heal humanity.

The co-conspirator's journey is our reminder that healing is the only path forward. When we continue to work from our wounded places, either ignoring or causing harm, we are only walking backward from our humanity and backward into our history. We are being drawn back into the pattern of our ancestors and our ancestral oppressors. When we move forward, we heal humanity. It's like the concept of *ubuntu*, an Nguni Bantu word from the people of Southern Africa, which means humanity toward others and is often translated to "I am because we are."

I am because we are.

The co-conspirator's journey begins with this awareness, followed by a call to action, and then requires us to face ourselves and our misdoings, including those that have brought us shame. The fear of shame can lead us to ghost the entire process, which is just another backward step into ancestral harm and complicity in imperialist, capitalist, and white supremacist racism.

Shame is an important part of the process. In order to be a true co-conspirator, we must turn the light on "shame" in order to sincerely grapple with the lessons we need to learn. Shame can be a catalyst and a teacher, but only if we move through it. Then, we can fail our way forward to heal. But fear of shame, or refusing to move through the actions it requires to unlearn those old supremacist tools, can lead to analysis paralysis, ultimately keeping well-intentioned co-conspirators from moving forward in their work and often leading them to ghost the process of growth.

Many co-conspirators get stuck in this phase of the journey. Have you ever been so caught up in your head thinking about the worst-case scenario that you freeze and become immobile to take the next step of action? The fear of getting it right leads to a freeze, and the freeze is so uncomfortable, it's just easier to flee than stay and fight alongside the people you were working to support. One co-conspirator I work closely with is a woman named Britney, a white wife and mother who runs an animal sanctuary in Georgia. Britney has been on her journey for three years and describes that freeze as "feeling trapped in a state of constant mental and emotional overwhelm, where self-doubt and fear turn to apathy, leaving me feeling powerless to do anything."

This experience of analysis paralysis took Britney down the path of ghosting her process. While ghosting is typically used as a dating term, in the context of the co-conspirator's journey, it occurs from the discomfort that arises when someone moves away the psychological and emotional safety with which most white folx in the United States and abroad live and are born. When our safety feels threatened, it is easier for us to emotionally "flee." Ghosting comes when we choose to stay comfortable. Comfort is not a teacher in life; discomfort offers the lessons we need to learn.

Our victory on this journey is waking up from comfort and reawakening to healing. And healing is not a comfortable journey. If you've ever broken a bone or sprained an ankle, you know healing can be more painful, uncomfortable, and frustrating than the original injury, and yet it is a biological requirement for recovery. Together, we are recovering the past and we are healing it forward.

Healing our epigenetic DNA will allow us to rewire our brains and face the memories of our ancestral past.

> When we heal the fourteen generations before
> us, we heal fourteen generations in the future.

When thinking about our ancestral past, two ideas come to mind: epigenetics and traumatic stress. I may not be the expert in either but what I know for sure is that what you fail to heal will show up and impact your relationships in a variety of ways.

According to the CDC, "Epigenetics is the study of how your behaviors and environment can cause changes that affect the way your genes work. Unlike genetic changes, epigenetic changes are reversible and do not change your DNA sequence, but they can change how your body reads a DNA sequence." From this definition we can see the benefits of changed behavior over time can impact the ways in which we take our healing journeys individually, and collectively.

In terms of trauma, Dr. Rachel Yehuda, director of the Traumatic Stress Studies Division at the Icahn School of Medicine at Mount Sinai in New York City, conducted a 2015 study on the children of forty Holocaust survivors. She found that they had epigenetic changes to a gene linked to their levels of cortisol, a hormone involved in the stress response. She also found a distinctive pattern of DNA methylation, another epigenetic marker. The study concluded that both parents and unborn children were affected on a genetic level.[1]

The co-conspirator's journey requires constant evaluation and interrogation. We must look at the stories of our ancestors, evaluating where they went wrong in order to finally make the buck stop here. It is a journey of choice and it requires a deep examination into the self, allowing us to thoroughly uncover the roots of who we are in hopes of showing up differently in the world. It is a journey similar to the hero's journey, wherein the ancestral hero goes on an adventure, struggles through an existential crisis in order to reach the goal and learn the lessons, before returning home and beginning the journey again.

This journey is a calling into purpose, to understand who we are called to be and why we are chosen to serve. We won't know the purpose of our journey until we take the first step into the unknown. The purpose of being co-conspirators is a courageous journey of serving others not just for the world we live in today—though that world certainly needs a whole lot of healing—but for our children and our children's children and our children's children's children.

> Purpose drives passion, and passion is what
> drives ongoing systemic change.

As a young girl growing up in the Christian church, I was taught I had a purpose. I learned that God had a plan for my life, and that scripture was the first step to "study and show ourselves approved." I can recall times seeing the women of the church in the kitchen cooking Sunday dinner, teaching Sunday school, and belting beautiful Black hymns from the church choir. While that was joyful to see, I knew it wasn't my purpose.

I believe we are born into the world to serve a purpose. This purpose is created from the moment of conception, from which we are born to bear witness and cultivate a world of new possibilities. From the moment we took our first breath, belched our first cry, our collective ancestors cheered as new life was given. From that moment forward we have been shaped by our parents, elders, and communities to walk into our purpose. As children we already have an innate knowledge of who we are to become in the world. We want to be doctors, teachers, preachers, writers. We all have a silent inner voice or gut instinct that directs us to the call that life purpose walks us into, which is why when I looked around that church pulpit, I knew what I was called to do.

I would listen to the pastors, predominantly men, speaking profound words, helping people navigate through life's challenges. In those moments I knew I was being called to do the same. As a young girl I knew that my purpose would be to empower people to get through life's difficulties. While the purpose felt impossible, I knew it was attainable. At least until I was told that women cannot lead in the church. At that moment my dreams of leading and teaching were crushed, and I was told that the purpose I thought was mine was only for men. I was taught that my purpose as a girl, and eventually a woman, would be to sit down and silently serve.

Even as young children, our beliefs in ourselves are shaped and socialized by the world around us. The adults, systems, and constructs teach us that we are not here to serve collective humanity but rather the oppressive systems in which we are born. And no matter who you are or where you come from, as long as you are participating in modern society, those systems are founded in misogyny, racism, imperialism, and a capitalist drive for wealth and power. And yet, in our own individual upbringings, we are taught either to hate or to love, to steal or to share resources, or to have power over or to have power with.

In a world striving for power over something, we have dismissed our original journey of life's purpose, instead perpetuating a smaller microcosm of those oppressive systems. In the powerful framework "The Cycle of Socialization," Bobbie Harro writes, "We are each born into a specific set of *social identities*, related to . . . categories of difference . . . and these social identities predispose us to unequal *roles* in the dynamic of systematic oppression."

Oppression is traditionally defined as "the social act of placing severe restrictions on an individual group, or institution."[2] We are all oppressed and we have all been taught to uphold oppression, which minimizes our ability to pursue our own identity and purpose toward personal and interpersonal development.

When we are living within an oppressive framework—when our decisions, choices, and life path are rooted in the ideals of the oppressor—we unconsciously cause harm in every aspect of our lives. Our interpersonal, professional, and personal relationships suffer as we continue to run on the hamster wheel of domination, of power *over* instead of power *with*. This wheel places value on perfectionism, performance, and keeping up with the Joneses over serving the liberation of ourselves and the greater collective. It's not until we have our great wake-up, or life shake-up, that we begin to unlearn and relearn the work we have always been called to do.

My great shake-up occurred when I realized that most of my relationships with white women were based on those women's need to rescue me from my life's trials and tribulations. Let me be clear and say there is a big difference between trying to rescue someone and offering healthy support in a friendship. A rescuer is driven to help others as a way to help themselves. Most white folx I encountered were rescuers. They couldn't sit with the pain that a Black woman with three children "had it so hard." Rather than be in a relationship with a Black woman, then on welfare, food stamps, and Section 8, they would give me things instead of sitting with me in my discomfort. They just wanted the comfort to go away. Rather than sit and listen, these white women wanted to fix me, my situation, and my children. Though helping people can be an important way to support each other, I was taken on like a project.

<blockquote>
Here is the thing:
A project is not a person.
</blockquote>

I realized that white women were attracted to my matriarchal nature of listening, nurturing, and supporting, but in return, they didn't provide the same support. They didn't know how to share a friendship based in security, boundaries, and love. They didn't want to share power; they wanted to use their resources to have power over me, my life, and my life choices. I realized the larger dynamic occurring between me and the white women in my life was rooted in the relationships developed three to four generations before and beyond, during the time of slavery.

Considering the times when Black women nursed the babies of white slave masters' wives, so the wives could have social status, I have felt like a wet nurse to white women, who demanded my energy. Many white women raised within patriarchal households cannot see how their relationship with oppression impacts their relationships with women of color.

My great shake-up helped me recognize the ways I had not only been socialized to uphold oppression but also to be an oppressor. I noticed a pattern of codependency rooted in ancestral trauma passed down generationally depending on how we were socialized into the world, and how I was voluntarily playing a role in a system created by the horrific violence and genocide against my ancestors. I didn't realize I had been socialized into whiteness until I recognized that my proximity to whiteness afforded me opportunities different from my Black counterparts. Since I grew up in a white suburb, with white peers, and went to good white schools, I was able to code-switch and code-interpret the world around me. I was so socialized into whiteness, I didn't even recognize my proximity to Blackness, even saying things like, "I feel sorry for those people," upon seeing enslaved Africans on slave ships.

DO NOW: Take a self-compassion break. As you are reading this, I am sure lots of conflicting thoughts are emerging. Dr. Kristin Neff defines *self-compassion* as acting the same way toward yourself when you are having a difficult time, fail, or notice something you don't like about yourself, as you would toward someone you love and care about. So go ahead and put a bookmark on the page and tell yourself, "I am going to be kind to myself right now. I am going to offer myself the same kindness I would offer someone I love." Step away from the book, maybe put it down for the day, and then pick it back up and keep going.

Waking up isn't just about being woke to the world in which we live, but truly reawakening to your life's purpose, to your reason to be here on this earth as a living, breathing entity in relationship with other living, breathing entities. It means to wake up to the collective energy and the spirit of the world that refuses to be broken despite our complicity in the systems into which we were born. When we are socialized into those systems, we have no choice but to lose our humanity. How can we participate in a system that generates so much violence, poverty, and death? Talk about paralysis. We relinquish our life purpose in order to please the people, places, and things that uphold the interlocking systems of our oppression.

I looked around that church as a child, and I was told I could not be the pastor. I was told my place was in the kitchen, serving the food, not serving the truth. And for many years after that, I lost my purpose in the name of those interlocking systems of domination known as imperialist, white supremacist, capitalist patriarchy. The first known description of this concept is found in the "Combahee River Collective Statement" (1977) by the Black feminist organization of the same name:

> The most general statement of our politics at the present time would be that we are actively committed to struggling against racial, sexual, heterosexual, and class oppression, and see as our particular task the development of integrated analysis and practice based upon the fact that the major systems of oppression are interlocking. The synthesis of these oppressions creates the conditions of our lives.[3]

My Black foremothers, elders, and ancestors knew that our true purpose can be actualized only through liberation from those systems of domination. But as many of us have learned, emancipation requires deep and committed work and effort. The system isn't interested in rewarding the people it wants to oppress, and it certainly doesn't reward them when they attempt to liberate themselves from the systems built to enslave them.

> The system rewards those who emulate it,
> who distance themselves from Blackness
> and intersectional feminism, who refuse to
> stand with the status quo and pretend it's
> a revolution.

Anti-Blackness is just one of the perpetual conditions designed by the system, and the system sees anything outside of its designated operating system as a threat, working to eliminate it by any means necessary. Our Black foremothers knew that the only way to be free from oppression was to liberate the entire collective. That none of us are free until all of us are free is a fact as true as $2 + 2 = 4$. The system wants us to prioritize the liberation of some over emancipation of the whole, but our healing journeys are forever bound to one another's, tracing back toward the past and reaching out into the future.

And on this healing journey we must interrogate and ask ourselves:

Are we aware of our conscious and unconscious biases and behaviors?

How are we sharing our resources to allow our liberation to be tied to one another?

Is it a privilege to seek joy on our journey?

Are we also making space for grief?

Do we seek joy and pleasure or are we constantly on the battlefield? Experiencing racial battle fatigue at every second?

So many questions and unknowns exist on this journey, and the truth is, there are some things we may never know. We won't be here for the end of the story. We are just at the beginning of the liberation story, and so we, or you as a white person, have to make space for the tension of non-closure. Because a witness always wants an answer, or proof via scientific methodologies, we reject scenarios that do not offer closure. The dominant systems require closure, which is why fairy tales must have happy endings, even after they project violence, death, and fear.

We are a culture of wanting answers on demand. When we can't get what we want, we run to Google, and when Google doesn't help, we ask our friends. If our friends don't tell us an answer, or the answer we want to hear, we keep searching outside ourselves to find closure. We are in an active state of denial, denying facts over fiction, and forcing rather than allowing. The truth is, part of healing means that we learn to allow the acceptance of non-closure, the key word being *acceptance*.

The Serenity Prayer serves as my constant reminder that acceptance is possible, moving beyond doubt and denial. The original Serenity Prayer was written by Karl Paul Reinhold Niebuhr, a white American Reformed theologian. Because I understand the nuances of patriarchy and Christianity, I've adapted the prayer in a way that is nonbinary and genderless:

Source/God/Higher Power/Community, grant me the serenity to accept the things I cannot change, the courage to change the things I can, and the wisdom to know the difference. Living one day at a time, enjoying one moment at a time, accepting hardship as a pathway to peace.

The reality is most folx don't want to accept the unknown or not have control of their life, choices, or decisions. However, in this work of healing trauma and repairing and moving forward in solidarity, we must allow ourselves the grace to get things wrong and allow things to be unresolved. You can't unlearn a lifetime of socialized beliefs in a day, but you can take continuous baby steps toward a new future, leaning into discomfort and the acceptance of non-closure. But this work requires self-awareness. If you aren't aware of how you, too, even with the best of intentions, are perpetuating oppression, you will continue to be a performative ally. I know it's a term that makes a lot of good white folx uncomfortable, but if we can't be aware of where we are working to alleviate perceptions rather than unlearn perceptions, it will never be conspiratorial, it will always be performative.

Waking up from performative allyship requires us all to drop into awareness. Like in the movie *The Matrix*, Neo saw the signs that something had to change. He dreamt of alternative universes and knew there was more to life than what he was living. Eventually he followed the white rabbit, which led him to Morpheus and the grave decision to wake up to awareness. In the famous blue pill/red pill scene, Morpheus is inviting Neo to a new level of consciousness:

Morpheus: "It is the world that has been pulled over your eyes to blind you from the truth."

Neo: "What truth?"

Morpheus: "That you are a slave, Neo. Like everyone else, you were born into bondage. Into a prison you cannot smell or taste or touch. A prison for your mind."

This conversation reminds me of the awakening of 2020, when BIPOC educators were informing allies of the racial reckoning that was taking place. Allies needed a deeper understanding that it wasn't just the murders of George Floyd and Breonna Taylor. It was about the matrix of oppression, a term coined by Dr. Patricia Hill Collins, that allowed for those murders. But in order to stop the violence of oppression, we must recognize that there are many different ways one might experience domination, facing many different challenges in which one obstacle, such as race, may overlap with other sociological features. Such things as race, age, and sex, may affect an individual in extremely different ways, in such simple cases as varying geography, socioeconomic status, or simply throughout time. While we may have many unique experiences, we often play out our individual oppression in our interpersonal relationships.

Like in *The Matrix*, the interlocking systems of oppression keep us on the hamster wheel of sameness. Anything seen as a disruption to the system must be terminated. So while many well-meaning white folx began their antiracism journey with good intentions, they were not willing to risk being seen outside of the lens of sameness. In a world where we all fight to be seen, the path of healing is often an isolating nonlinear path that many are not willing to take. No matter how many times educators have told folx liberation is the goal, folx choose to be prisoners to what feels comfortable rather than leaning into the awareness of discomfort that comes with an awakening.

REFLECTION QUESTIONS ON THE CO-CONSPIRATOR'S JOURNEY

· · · · · ·

1. What does healing look like for you?

2. When thinking of ways you uphold oppression in your own life, what do you want to learn to let go of? If liberation is the goal, what are you doing to actively liberate yourself from the constructs of imperialist, white supremacist, capitalist patriarchy?

3. Are you treating BIPOC folx in your life as a project? How do you know? What are you willing to change?

· 2 ·

YOUR GREAT WHITE AWAKENING

"Your willingness to look at your darkness
is what empowers you to change."
—Iyanla Vanzant

To awaken is to notice an act or moment that brings you into greater awareness. At any given moment, we can be called to what is known as a Great Awakening—those shifts of consciousness where our perspective is radically altered, where we become ready to accept and let go of what no longer serves us. Often this awakening is born from the darkest moments of our lives, reminding us that in order to shift, change, and grow, we need to challenge our current understanding of and engagement with the here and now. We must become self-aware of what is. It is an invitation to let go of the habits that have kept us from stepping into our own healing.

When I think of awakening, I am referring to that exact moment when you know that something has to give, the moment some call "rock bottom," where your mental health is so impacted by grief, shock, despair, or desolation that you find yourself staring at the red pill or the blue pill, knowing that you must make the decision to change. Like Neo, or Alice in Wonderland before him, this rock bottom is in fact our great opportunity to see how our world is just a construct, a matrix of socialized ideas. You are reborn into a new reality, which might feel harsher at first as you realize that justice and equality are not for all, and that you have not been the "good white person" you always imagined yourself to be. In that moment, it is easy to go down a despair tunnel, recognizing your role in the violence you always believed was someone else's fault. But there is also something else there, another path, which shows you a more authentic world—not one filled with color-blind toxic positivity—but real lives, real hope, and, yes, real magic.

Can you name the moment of your awakening? Which Black life had to die so that you could awaken to the reality of Black lives not mattering? Was it the murder of Mike Brown, Trayvon Martin, Sandra Bland, Tamir Rice, Eric Garner, Lexi, Tony Mc-Dade, or George Floyd? Maybe those names aren't familiar to you, or maybe they weren't your catalyst.

> Maybe your awakening was far more
> personal—maybe injustice or violence
> impacted someone you know, a friend, a
> partner, a coworker, a child—
> or maybe you were the perpetrator.

Whatever the case, something shook you so hard to your core, you recognized your divine calling, awakening you to the inherent upholding of white culture, dominant ethnic socialization, and the interlocking systems of oppression. As a white person, you must understand that in the West, your culture, lifestyle, social groups, mindset, and religious upbringing are considered and idealized by the dominant systems as the "normal way of life." Any cultural group outside of whiteness, any behavior, ideology, religion, or systemic belief seen outside of that dominant culture, is viewed as inferior or abnormal.

Here's an example for ya: As a Black woman born to a single mother, I lived in a household and was raised with my mother and a grandmother who took care of me, while my mom worked. Growing up in the Bay Area suburb of Concord, most of my white peers saw my life as abnormal. Not many folx lived with their grandparents. In fact, most of their grandparents had legacy money that was handed down to their parents and then to them. So even if their parents seemed like they were "poor," there was always access to capital, somehow, by someone.

But for me, matriarchal households were the norm, especially being raised partially in Chicago. It wasn't abnormal to see my Black friends at church, at school, or in the neighborhoods with their mommas or big mommas. As I got older, I noticed how matriarchal culture was dominant throughout the Midwest, East Coast, and the South. But on the West Coast, specifically fakewoke California, from UC Berkley to SoCal suburbia, matriarchy wasn't even seen in the second wave feminist movement.

Concord, California, was where most whites moved to in the 1960s to get away from the ghettos of Oakland. In 1985, a Black man was found hanged at a Concord BART station. Authorities ruled the hanging a suicide, which shouldn't surprise anyone. One year later, an alleged member of the KKK was convicted on one count of assault after stabbing two Black men at a Halloween party. Moving to Concord less than ten years later, it would come as no surprise that my Blackness would be seen as inferior. As a young Black woman in suburbia, it wasn't normal to have full lips and wide hips. Most of the white boys teased me for my appearance and lobbied other degrading terms at me that challenged my Black existence. So many of today's Black girls are still fighting to be seen in a system that elevates their peers but keeps them ashamed for being in their full humanity.

Even though kids were cruel to me, I learned to charge it to their hearts and not their heads. This taught me that white folx would be nice if I "let it go"; in return, I was buying into the supremacy and normalcy of whiteness and white identity. The idea that I spent my life degrading my own identity enforced my colonial mentality as an oppressed person. A colonial mentality is "the internalized attitude of ethnic or cultural inferiority felt by people as a result of colonization, i.e. them being colonized by another group."[1] It corresponds with the belief that the cultural values of the colonizer are inherently superior to one's own.

Understanding what I know now, many of my white peers were socialized through family and media to see me as nothing more than the help. I was a young girl who didn't have the small frame, blonde hair, and blue eyes that would mark me as one of the popular girls. Even as I write this, I can hear a voice in my head whispering, "Well, not all white people treated me this way." Because the truth is, I did have friends who did their best to be an ally for me. However, I now know that my internal struggle with whiteness was driven by the allyship being offered, one steeped in the colorblind rhetoric of high-end millennials who "didn't see color" and who positioned their own multiethnicity without really connecting it into their own ethnic backgrounds.

My white peers, like most socialized to American culture, have all been impacted by what researchers are now calling racial socialization, which "refers to the process by which parents transmit both implicit and explicit messages about the meaning of one's race in a broader societal context."[2] In short, your level of awareness of the interlocking systems of oppression is based on the ways in which information was externally transmitted, verbally and nonverbally, consciously and unconsciously. According to scholars, there are four types of racialized socialization that impact how children can learn to socialize racially. I believe this newer framework helps adults understand how we have come to see the world:

- Cultural socialization: Practices in which parents engage to teach their children how to navigate cultural spaces and teach cultural pride, like through dance or movement or art.
- Preparation for bias: Practices that parents use to help their children understand what racial bias looks like as well as strategies to cope with it.
- Promotion of mistrust: Practices parents use to teach their child to be cautious of interracial interactions.
- Egalitarianism: Practices that parents employ to teach their children that all people are created equal and that racism is not a problem.

Your parents' external influences, social beliefs, past beliefs, and behaviors were all shaped by the influences, beliefs, and behaviors of their parents, and their parents before them.

> When we think of how far back culture and learned belief systems extend in a family system, we begin to understand the generational imprint of racism throughout our bloodlines and also our society.

These inherited beliefs have caused unconscious implicit attitudes around how you see and understand race and identity. Your behavioral beliefs shape your norms and are then expressed verbally and nonverbally. So if your family had Black women around only as the nanny or the help, you may have internalized Black women as your sense of emotional safety. If your family never had you in proximity to marginalized people of color, you were shaped by what you saw via media, caregiver bias, and other peers on how to interpret folx who don't hold a dominant identity. This transmission of behaviors is why today even young white children will tease my children on the playground, including Latino children, who having assimilated to whiteness, comfortably calling my oldest child a nigger.

You are what your environment produces you to see, know, do, and learn, and as Maya Angelou says, once we learn better, we can then do better. You have a responsibility to awaken awareness to heal the seven generations forward as well as the seven generations behind. Because once we are able to see a different future, we want to heal the past, we want to shine a bright light on those inherited influences, beliefs, and behaviors. We want to remove the imprint of racism that has been branded into each of our souls, coloring the way we look at each other and how we view the world.

Awakening to whiteness, oppression, and racial perpetuation is a challenging and difficult process. Similar to the cycle of the butterfly, the radical transformation required is necessary to the journey. Healer and author Vince Gowmon suggests this transformation occurs by way of "1) Leaving the known and comfortable; 2) Incubation and dissolution of self; 3) Emergence of the enlightened butterfly."[3]

But let's be real, we aren't always enlightened on this journey, because life is a demanding-enough process without enlighten-ment. We have bills to pay and kids to feed and romance issues to deal with and pandemics to live through. But just like the butter-fly, sometimes, we are just inching along the ground, and other times, we are soaring into the sky.

The butterfly has a life cycle of four stages—egg, caterpillar, chrysalis, and butterfly—but for the sake of our conversation, we're going to hone in on the caterpillar and chrysalis. The cat-erpillar stage is known as the feeding stage, where according to the Academy of Natural Sciences at Drexel University, "The job of the caterpillar is to eat and eat and eat. As the caterpillar grows it splits its skin and sheds it about 4 or 5 times. Food eaten at this time is stored and used later as an adult. Caterpillars can grow 100 times their size during this stage."

DO NOW: Stop reading and start breathing. Four-Seven-Eight Breathing is a practice to reduce anxiety or stress. Conversations on race aren't easy, but breathwork is a practice that allows you to drop into yourself and into the softer places of our understand-ing. So, take a big exhale and empty the lungs of air. Breathe in quietly through the nose for four seconds and hold the breath for a count of seven seconds. Then, exhale forcefully through the mouth, pursing the lips and making a "whoosh" sound for eight seconds, repeating the cycle up to four times.

When you first awaken on your antiracist journey, you begin to consume information. In fact, you are likely going to overconsume information to a point where you get so full you can't take it any-more. This is the stage of reading all the books, listening to the podcasts, following every blue-check intersectional expert, prov-ing you're a good white person. It is in this stage of awareness you have two choices: eat until you're full and give up, or consume the food and go within. If you choose to go within, then you are ready for the second stage, which is chrysalis. Known as the pupa stage, which can last weeks, months, or even longer, this stage looks like nothing is happening, but on the inside, big things are poppin'. For the butterfly, cells are growing rapidly and eventually turning into the parts that produce the butterfly. It is the sum of these parts that produces the greatest stages of transformation, but it is also the most difficult stage. Do you think it is easy or comfortable or even painless to go from a homely caterpillar to sprouting wings and becoming a butterfly? Hell no. This is hard work.

Most co-conspirators avoid this stage because giving up a right to comfort is, well, uncomfortable. Even the most well-meaning white people are addicted to privilege. We saw this with the Great White Awakening of 2020 where we saw the world react to witnessing the murder of our ancestors George Floyd, Breonna Taylor, and transgendered folx Lexi and Tony McDade. White people rallied on social media, posted black squares, and gave money, but what most folx didn't realize is that justice requires total transformation.

The 2021 terrorist attack on the US Capitol proved that 2020 was the greatest white performance in history. White folx stepped back into the caterpillar stage of awareness, rejecting the chrysalis that would have led to real change and growth.

Sure, people were horrified. There were easy analogies to the violence and force used against BLM protestors just seven months before, and yet, there was barely a movement toward any action. Where were the white folx when they watched their own attack the Capitol? Where were the demands for justice? Where was the real work for change? Now, if you're reading this book right now, I am sure you are thinking to yourself, *I did something. I (posted about it). I (cried about it). I (was shocked/angry/horrified/upset).*

But I'm not asking what your reaction was. What was your action? What actions did you take to show the world that this is not who your people are? What actions are you taking today to show the world such terrorism will not be tolerated?

In my online community, the Co-Conspirators Lounge, I have witnessed how white folx can lean into the chrysalis stage, understanding the deep-rooted growth required to shift into action and into the constant cycle of change. What we have discovered is that most of our deeper practices require the support of licensed mental health professionals to unlearn, relearn, and re-imagine what levels of awareness are needed to heal.

As one of the members of my community, licensed social worker Kerrie Mohr, of A Good Place Therapy, says:

> The fundamental goal of therapy is enhanced self-understanding. Growing up in a society with a baked-in Euro-patriarchal worldview means that we internalize these ideas and illusions about ourselves, the world, and other people. Dismantling these ingrained views is the great work in front of us. Our beliefs determine how we perceive and experience events in our lives. Exploring these beliefs in a critical way sheds light on these belief systems, which may have been previously assumed and unspoken.
>
> We must create distance from these beliefs and examine the ways they serve us, but also harm us and the people around us. Then, we can learn ways to shift, to question, and to make changes in our lives. We can and must live in alignment with our higher values.

It can be challenging to have our understanding of the world challenged, and it's easy to feel powerless in the face of violence and terrorism, which is so easy to other. *Those people are responsible, but not my people.* But we are responsible for our communities. It is that old capitalist system that tells us otherwise, teaches us to pull ourselves up from our bootstraps and not ask for help, and similarly, not to offer help.

> **It's easier to call for justice than it is to enact it, especially when enacting it would disrupt the privilege and comfort of the white worldview.**

As Kerrie Mohr shares, "The privileged white worldview feels safe and just. Systems work in our favor. We have certainty in knowing clearly what is right and what is wrong, but when we start to do antiracism work, we inevitably learn that what we think is right is in fact wrong."

In 2012, I went through my own personal awareness journey. It was so uncomfortable, it led me to a seven-day hospitalization for suicide ideation with a plan. In one of the darkest moments of my life, I had lost my will to live. Not wanting to be seen as another "welfare queen," a single mom with three kids, I had been pushed to my limits by patriarchal and Westernized Christian societal standards. My church raised me to believe that it was a sin to have sex before marriage. Society raised me to believe it was a sin to be a single mother. The government raised me to believe I was a leech on the resources it would barely dole out. Now, I can understand that each of those institutions were rooted in misogyny and racism and, honestly, plain old meanness. But at the time, I didn't have the language to put these ideologies into perspective, instead falling down a shame spiral and toward a path of death. It was during my hospitalization that I began to understand the power of therapy and how peer support could help me on my journey forward.

At one point I recall telling my pastor, "If only I felt that I had peers to relate to, I would not have gotten to the point of wanting to take my life. When I leave this place, I am going to start something for Black women to not feel isolated in life."

It was that moment of awareness that made we realize that Black women needed spaces where they could speak freely. But in order to enter awareness, I first needed to fail forward in life. And that moment became the beginning of my ongoing healing journey.

I tell awakening folx that in order to stay safe, committed, and supported in their awareness on this journey, they need three things: peer support, relationships with other folx on the same healing path as them, and therapy. Now, I understand that it is a privilege to have access to therapy, and it may not be financially accessible for all, but you can often find formal peer groups that will provide similar benefits, offering compassionate feedback and holding space for the tough stuff that is bound to come up when you do this work. And there will be tough stuff.

> **Story is sacred, and seeing yourself in someone's story helps us all heal.**

If you are able to access therapeutic options, there are many modalities that can actively and positively support your co-conspirator journey, including cognitive behavior therapy (CBT), dialectical behavioral therapy (DBT), eye movement desensitization and reprocessing (EMDR), and internal family systems

(IFS). All these can be effective for identifying pain points on the journey. I believe the best and most effective therapies to try on this journey are EMDR and IFS.

I have especially seen the positive impacts of IFS on my own life and on members of the Co-Conspirators Lounge, and it's no surprise. In order to move into awareness, we need to visit the family stories that keep us prisoner from freeing ourselves from the entanglements of our inherited oppression. And trust me, no matter who you are, if you are living in the twenty-first century, you have inherited oppression. Oppression is a spectrum—some of us come from the oppressor, some come from the oppressed, some of us come from both. But IFS helps us identify our multiple parts, to discover who we truly are, who we come from, and the work we need to embark upon in order to change, heal, and grow.

So let's talk about internal family systems for a second. First off, I'm not a licensed therapist, so don't take this as medical or even therapeutic advice. However, I am a mental health advocate and survivor and I have seen how IFS has helped me step into myself, taking responsibility for my past, present, and future. I acknowledge the impacts of trauma but I also take full responsibility for consciously living my life.

If you are able to work in IFS, you will begin to create awareness around these multiple—and often conflicting—parts and stories that make up your human experience. It is how we feel outright horror at the murder of George Floyd (because we know that murder is wrong and watching any of that footage struck at a core belief system that we should not kill one another) and yet may also not be able to fully show up as an ally when we watch the terrorist attack on the Capitol (because we have also been raised to "other" people who don't hold our views even if we actually benefit from the worldview those "other" people are trying to uphold). When these parts come into conflict, it's almost as if our worldview short-circuits. Otherwise supportive allies get lost in their own good work, and it's easier to back away than to push through the incongruity that is human nature.

I want to acknowledge that IFS was created by a psychotherapist named Richard Schwartz, a white cisgender male. However, he has been very open and expressive about his ongoing self-interrogation regarding his complicity with supremacy. What Dr. Schwartz did understand was that by helping people make sense of those multiplicity of parts, they could stand more firmly in their identity and in their body. By honoring myself and my incongruent parts, I am able to see the truth.

According to Dr. Schwartz, IFS is rooted in "helping people first access their Self and, from that core, come to understand and heal their parts." IFS creates inner and outer connectedness, which I believe allows a synergetic connection between the mind, body, and spirit, grounding its participants in humanity and helping them understand that they are greater than the sum of their parts.

The IFS model includes addressing four parts of the human self: the manager self, the firefighter self, the exiled self, and the core self. Our manager self shows up on the scene like the annoying supervisor who is always wanting perfection to help drive the bottom line. The manager runs your daily life and uses self-sufficiency as the key driver of fulfillment, making sure that you are productive in your 9-to-5 role.

The firefighter self is the first responder on an emergency scene. They respond well to crises, providing assistance during emergencies. The firefighter follows a strict protocol to protect and help somebody experiencing an emergency situation. Not surprisingly, we see a lot of these parts walking around co-conspirator land, always rushing in when there is an emergency but not showing up to help prevent the fire in the first place.

The job of the firefighter self is to show up and numb the exiled self with distractions. The exiled self wants to be seen and heard but is afraid. The exiled self has been pushed down and hidden, believing that vulnerability is a weakness rather than a strength. But more than anything, the exiled self wants to reunite with the core self.

The core self is full of compassion and curiosity and a playful, childlike nature of love. The core self is full of life and needs no fixing, only the self-permission to show up and be itself.

According to IFS theory, these systems help us understand that "everyone has a Self, and the Self can and should lead the individual's internal system. As we develop, our parts develop and form a complex system of interactions among ourselves . . . Changes in the internal system will affect changes in the external system and vice versa."

When I came to see how the integration of IFS could help one make sense of the world around and within them, it felt as if I had finally found the answer to a question bell hooks once posed and which had long lived in me: "How do we hold people accountable for wrongdoing and yet at the same time remain in touch with their humanity enough to believe in their capacity to be transformed?"

We can hold people accountable for the
work they have to do on themselves—that
deep inner work—while also reminding them of
the work they are responsible for in the
outside world.

When learning from a method of integration, white folx (and all folx) are able to drop deeper into themselves and access those inner parts, which are the barriers to outward change. But for white co-conspirators, integration to self-awareness can help you move from performative allyship to compassionate action. As co-conspirator Kerrie Mohr shared:

> Every great awakening is an invitation to look at our darkness and begin to see the light within. When we wake up to whiteness, and white socialized behavior, we see the ways in which our past and parts hinder our journey forward. As you awaken you must give yourself grace to get things wrong and get them wrong often. With each mistake you learn a lesson necessary to support the growth that is needed and necessary for the journey ahead.

And this work is truly about the journey ahead for all of humanity. At this rate, we won't have much of a planet left for our future generations to enjoy. Being a radical and loving co-conspirator means being a powerful ally for the people and the planet, by showing up and moving from the inner work into powerful acts of change, growth, and resistance. The incredible side effect of all this growth is that as we move deeper into self-compassion, we move deeper into self-love, and I'm not talking about the look at yourself in the mirror, #livelovelaugh kind of self-love. No, I am talking about loving your humanness so much, you love all humanness, and you become committed to saving it.

Iyanla Vanzant reminds us that the first step toward radical healing is the moment we start looking at ourselves. So this is it, this is your moment. Go ahead and look. What do you see?

REFLECTION QUESTIONS ON
THE GREAT WHITE AWAKENING

· · · · · ·

1. Do you believe that you can see yourself in someone's story? How has that informed your journey?

2. Take a few moments and think of the last time you felt heard. Who was listening? Where were you? What feelings or sensations do you remember feeling in your body?

3. How often are you listening to fix someone, rather than sit with their individual truth?

4. Have you considered therapy or peer support groups for your journey? What has worked? What has not?

· 3 ·

THERE IS ROOM FOR WHITE TEARS

"Grief does not change you, Hazel. It reveals you."
—John Green

There is room for white tears.

Yup, I said it. In fact, it might just be one of the most controversial things a Black woman can say, but guess what? It's time we break the patriarchal notion that grief is for babies. We need to challenge the notion that we must pull ourselves up by our bootstraps and pretend as if our complex human emotions don't exist. Outside the scope of race and binary thinking, we must begin to process that white folx also need grief to do this work. I *am not* saying that POC need to be the ones to hold space for that grief, but what I am saying is that white folx need to understand why grief is necessary for the healing journey, for *their* healing journey.

Imperialist, capitalist, ableist, and white supremacist patriarchy is the embodiment of "suck it up" culture. Deny your feelings and keep on keeping on. What I love about growing up in a Black matriarchal culture is how it recognizes grief as a necessity, allowing for sadness, but also for the humanity of moving forward. I once preached on a series called "The Gifts of the Black Church" where I shared, "I am the prayer and the tears of the ancestors who knew something better was to come. Their grief made space for me to come alive, they worked, cried, and prayed for me into existence. Had it not been for their collective grief and *belief,* I don't know if I could stand before you and speak." And now, write.

If as a white person, you continue to deny the space for your grief on this journey, you will continue to perform, perpetuate, and polarize yourself in your soul's work. You might not recognize grief right away. The fact is, if you've spent a lot of time in a state of doing, reading, researching, posting, and podcasting, you probably haven't made space to sit and process what you think, feel, and desire. Maybe, right now, you're even feeling like this is just another tick box on your never-ending co-conspirator to-do list. Read the book, watch the video, feel the grief, and done, right? No.

The idea of hyperperformance and getting things done for the sake of saying you did it is not only not helpful, it's harmful. Most movements fail because folx aren't spending time truly understanding the humanity of their work—from the jobs that pay to the deeper inner journeys we all take on the path to being human. Since most white folx respond only to trauma and pain rather than being self-compassionate and present for the ongoing journey ahead, they will wait for a detrimental moment to happen, and like clockwork, they will show up, sign petitions, rally, take workshops, and check the checkbox of being antiracist.

But that's just more doing, and doing is the opposite of awareness. Awareness is an inner process of facing yourself and auditing not just the world and the systems within it, but yourself. A self-audit requires you to begin the integration of this work. Rooting yourself in self-compassion, you begin to interrogate your identity, friends, choices, and the power you have to be proximate and support others. You might start with evaluating the intellect—your thoughts, values, and belief systems—but ultimately, the deeper research is found in your heart, which is the true inspiration for radical action. We can know something is unjust but when we feel it in our hearts, we are moved into action.

> This is why we must address our grief. We must stop and feel the pain in our chest, the burn in our belly, the tears in our eyes.

If we are constantly checking boxes, we aren't offering ourselves the space we need to not just understand this work, but also connect into its deepest purpose.

When you recognize the audit as part of the process, you can see the necessity of grief on your journey forward. Often, being a co-conspirator requires white folx to lose a part of who they were, even if it's a part of themselves that brings up sadness or shame.

In 2019, I was preparing for a workshop entitled "Radical Self Compassion in a White Supremacist World." I knew that white folx had been indoctrinated to not hold space in this work to feel or grieve, let alone cry. In fact, I was told by many that white folx were too exhausting to have a conversation with on compassion. I constantly pushed back because, honestly, we're all exhausting. I know I'm exhausting to my partner and, shit, kids are exhausting to all of us. This rhetoric around what white folx do and don't deserve drove me all the more to want to hold a workshop on what it means to be compassionate, what it means to be human, and ultimately, what it means to struggle with the ideology of "not all white people."

I was explaining the workshop to one of my teachers, as I wanted to use it as a stand-alone project for my senior thesis. She told me that I was onto something, but the one thing that was needed was a "space for white tears." As my professor said, "How revolutionary would that be?"

I remember hearing her thoughts and saying to myself, *What the hell? No one is holding space for my perpetual pain navigating the world as a Black woman in society. What do I look like holding space for white folx's pain?*

But then I remembered an experience I had recently had at my job at the church. Bringing church into a conversation about anti-racist frameworks is probably taboo, but I'm gonna take a chance here and use it as a teachable lesson. If Christianity isn't for you, well, then we have something in common because it's not for me either. Let's just say, I am sharing my insight for "science."

There was a time I was undergoing a process to co-lead the deacons' board at a multiracial church. The goal of the deacons' board was to make unbiased and supportive decisions to help the church and community members in crisis. Part of the process was reading Acts 2: 42–47 (New International Version) about the ideology of "fellowshipping as believers." In this part of the Bible, it talks about folx finding common humanity: breaking bread together, praying, being in community, offering mutual aid, selling their possessions and giving them away, and creating a fellowship among all people. I began to realize that collective liberation meant that I too would need to learn the radical necessity of being in community with folx whose common belief was healing and building new systems.

Who was I to decide whether white folx could
or should have space to grieve if, at the end of
the day, all of human experience and humanity
is tied to one another's liberation?

Let me be clear and say, don't put this expectation on other marginalized persons of color. A lot of white folx will take this work literally and begin triangulating POC's work against one another's. We are not your space to grieve, but that doesn't mean you shouldn't find and create your own space to hold the tears that you too deserve on your journey.

I argue with folx all the time about the necessity of white grief on the journey of healing. Some folx tell me I'm crazy for even believing that I owe white people my time and space to grieve. We forget that two things can be true at the same time: Yes, white folx can be problematic and harmful as hell *and* still, everyone deserves the right to have their humanity. All I know is this: We are constantly evolving as human beings, and if we don't allow space for folx to grieve, we are only continuing to perpetuate and duplicate systems of oppression.

And those systems—you know, the good old imperialist, capitalist, white supremacist, and patriarchal ones—don't want us to be liberated. They are rooted in maintaining the way the systems function, having power over others, and leaving little to no space for vulnerability. Instead, they monopolize on the pain and suffering of others. This is why the dominant culture is rooted in individualism. It pushes you to look away, pull yourself up by your bootstraps, and reject the pain, the shame, and the vulnerability. It requires that you reject community because it is in community that we heal. And you know what a healed society looks like, don't you? It's not having to buy shit off the internet in order to feel better, it's not so scared and lonely and depressed that it doesn't have the energy to speak up and fight for justice, it's not so starved and overworked that it doesn't have the time to give a damn. A healed society is dangerous.

That's why dominator culture did not give a damn when my ancestors were stolen from their homeland, separated, forced into chattel enslavement, and offered no space to grieve, even centuries later, when they were finally freed. Dominator culture doesn't care that thousands of girls under the age of seventeen go missing in Mexico every year. And for sure, dominator culture doesn't care about missing and murdered Black trans women and men. Dominator culture is responsible for their deaths.

As a co-conspirator, you have a responsibility to give a damn. But in order to truly give that damn, you have to break up with dominator culture and move into a cycle of grief necessary to heal your way forward. I don't know who taught you that your feelings didn't matter, but until you take space to grieve, you can't show up well, and certainly not in the right way.

So, let's unpack grief for a second. According to *Psychology Today*, grief in white American culture is defined as "the acute pain that accompanies loss. Because it is a reflection of what we love, it can feel all-encompassing. Grief is not limited to the loss of people, but when it follows the loss of a loved one, it may be compounded by feelings of guilt and confusion, especially if the relationship was a difficult one." In white culture, we see that grief is usually rooted in the loss of people, but in my culture, we see death as a liberation of the sufferings of life and the celebration of one's homegoing, which is a return to the origins of one's soul.

Across cultures, grief and grief ceremonies appear different and yet attempt to offer a ritual or practice to help the grieved surrender to the feelings of loss, releasing tension, and restoring the continuity of relationships. Among the Dagara people of Burkina Faso, West Africa, grief rituals are conducted regularly within tribes and are offered to children as soul-cleansing rites to nurture and nourish their souls. In American culture, we often see the practice of grief as something outside of ourselves that is temporarily faced. James Baldwin said it best: "Not everything that is faced can be changed, but nothing can be changed until it is faced."

Grief is natural; grief is a practice.

Right now, you may be wondering, *Great, but what exactly am I grieving for? My ancestors were the ones who caused the pain. They enslaved Africans.* Maybe you're thinking, *But I have grieved. I wasn't one of those people who didn't see color until Breonna Taylor was murdered.* Or you may just believe that your suffering doesn't matter because only marginalized lives matter. I cannot tell you what you can or cannot believe, however I can encourage you to radically challenge your own narrative.

You have a lot to grieve on this journey. For starters, let's talk about the loss of identity. So many co-conspirators find themselves in an ongoing identity crisis. Think about it. When you were born, all the cards were placed on the table, creating an anticipated outcome for your life. If you were born with "the invisible knapsack of privilege," then everything—and I mean everything—is working to your advantage. You likely grew up not even considering how your racialized identity made space for you to have access to everything you have experienced in life. There's a good chance you grew up hearing "we don't see color." Seeing a Black person at your predominately white school was likely considered normal; you were probably friends, even good or best friends, with people of color. Despite any personal hardships (and most everyone has personal hardships), you may have aced the SATs, got a four-year scholarship, and landed a great job after college. Though you may have undergone mental and physical trauma, you also had access to healing through therapy and spiritual direction. The childhood grief may not have been handled as a child, but as you adapted to adulthood, you had the privilege to access the necessary resources and healing tools needed to persist in moving forward. You succeeded through life maintaining your colorblind attitude, not recognizing that you had color to thank for everything.

DO NOW: Cry. Make space to honor where you are in process and honor your need to grieve. Allowing yourself to cry will create room for space to receive messages that guide your healing process forward.

As a white person born with this unseen privilege, it is far past the time to recognize that your access, accomplishments, and accolades came at the cost of oppressing others. You may not see it clearly, but depending on where you are on your journey, you can slowly see how the life you once thought was a bed of roses was driven to uphold and enforce imperialist, white supremacist, capitalist patriarchy. In order to fully integrate into this work, you need to slow down and grieve because you are not only losing a worldview but also the way you have experienced your own life. You have awakened to the ideology that life is not what it seems. The old identity must experience grief to fully embody the calling toward a reparative future.

When I first began Check Your Privilege, I didn't start it from a place of success or a goal-driven strategy; it came from grief.

Check Your Privilege led me down the path of identity politics and into my own discomfort. I had to ask myself who I was and begin to face the truth and radical honesty of not knowing. I had to spend weeks and months in therapy, seeking a therapist who looked like me and could speak to my experience. I had to read books and articles and listen to podcasts to help deepen my understanding of African spirituality and the Black American experience. It was in my own learning and unlearning that I found that grief was the teacher and I was a student. I was a student learning real history and the dynamics of cross-cultural relationships. I had to grieve, and continue to grieve, my socializations and my past and current relationships. I had to forgive myself and others for upholding the systemic oppression that works against all of us.

Check Your Privilege was an invitation for me to lean into my work, and it took pain and purpose for me to get here. I still grieve, I still wrestle with my identity, but the more I step into myself, the process gets easier and I can see my way over and through the losses that are an integral part of growth and healing— and not beat myself up for not letting go sooner.

You must also realize that you are likely grieving more than the loss of identity; you will also be grieving relationships that no longer support you. In this work a lot of white folx spend time asking their friends, mothers, fathers, siblings, and partners to join them on the journey, and many are met with pain and disdain and rejection. This leaves folx to question the practice of becoming antiracist. It's not surprising that when folx don't feel supported, they then give up before barely getting started. It's not ghosting the journey per se, but rather a result of the bandwagon effect, which occurs when a larger group of cognitive biases influence an individual's judgment. But biases serve a purpose—

they are a shortcut to understanding the human experience, even if they often also result in mistakes and miscalculations.[1]

Essentially many white folx who leave the journey do so because they don't feel supported by their immediate family, friends, or social support systems, and the discomfort of that potential rejection is too much to handle. Many white people don't want to feel like a white traitor, so they continue to perform and not drop into letting go of people who don't want to take the same path forward as them. Bandwagon effect and groupthink biases serve as powerful reminders that who we surround ourselves with can contribute to the outcomes and goals we have set for ourselves.

> If you are truly committing to the work,
> you begin to realize that you gotta let go of
> not just certain people but also the notion
> that you can convince those people to take
> the journey with you.

Not everyone is ready to fully commit to this work, and trying to convince others to join you is fighting against a current. Once you recognize that folx don't wanna go, you must keep moving forward. This grief might feel like loss of life, you may feel like you are violating a bond between you and your family or friends, but that cycle of grief, and the stories that will come with it, will subside. It's why there is space for white people and white women's tears in this work. Because there should be loss, there should be grief, there should be a deep and unsettling rejection of what was in order to embrace what can be.

DO NOT WEAPONIZE YOUR TEARS

You can grieve *without* weaponizing your tears. Weaponizing tears is when white people, mainly women, employ grief "to muster sympathy and avoid accountability, by turning the tables on their accuser." Many people are unconsciously aware of when they are doing this, although some use it more intentionally because they know our culture of whiteness prioritizes the psychological and emotional safety and comfort of white folx over all others.

In the past, when I have told a white person that they have caused harm to me, it is often met with shock, denial, anger, and dismissiveness. And then it moves to me being gaslit, the space in which the person's denial is so big, I second-guess my own mental health based on what I felt I experienced. This cycle, often known as the Karpman Drama Triangle, becomes even more nuanced when race is added to the process. This triangle is a destructive interaction that can occur among folx in conflict. Whenever I told someone in a workplace that I experienced harm, more often the tables would get turned, and I would be written up rather than the person who harmed me, who themselves would express feeling threatened or disrespected if my "tone" was deemed inappropriate.

But even beyond my personal experience, we have seen white tears weaponized against black folx across history. In 1955, Carolyn Bryant, a twenty-one-year-old white woman from the South, accused fourteen-year-old Emmet Till, a Black boy from Chicago, of flirting with her. Four days later, his body was found in the Tallahatchie River. He had been beaten, mutilated, shot in the head, and drowned. His mother held his funeral with an open casket so the world could see.

Fifty-two years later, Carolyn Bryant admitted the incident never happened, and justice for Emmet Till still has not been won.

In 2020, Quawan Charles, a fifteen-year-old Black boy, was found dead in a sugar cane field in Iberia Parish, Louisiana. Quawan had gone out with a white family. He was reported missing before they discovered his body days later. The mother of the family cried when accusations of murder came upon her, and to this day, neither she nor her family have been held accountable for Quawan's death.

While these stories are extreme, you can see that when a white person merely plays the role of "victim," it discredits hearing all sides of the story. You can also see how your tears can be used to avoid accountability for the harm that has been caused. Crying gives you a pass to perpetuate violence and not take ownership of the harm caused. This is the danger of using your tears as a weapon—essentially, it makes it safe for you to carry on and live unconsciously, while marginalized folx suffer in silence.

Another note is that systems of oppression love the binary of virtue, of goodness and evil. Most of us are socialized to uphold this binary, so being held accountable feels like an attack on our goodness. These intense feelings cause bouts of guilt and denial, which then cause us to project our feelings onto others. If everyone is a mirror, then oftentimes what we see in others is what we are still healing in ourselves. Being called out is an intense moment on your journey. In response, you can choose to project your shame, fear, guilt, and tears onto others, projecting your lack of self-accountability onto marginalized people of color, or you can learn to practice a pause so your tears aren't harmful. If you don't practice a pause when being called in, you set yourself up for "damsel in distress" syndrome, requiring that someone save you from what you don't want to face.

When a person of color tells you they are harmed, pause and believe them. Remember you are not a victim on this journey, you are simply an imperfect and flawed human doing your best. When you refuse to play the victim, leaning into discomfort instead, you make space for the teachable moments, which is how we heal along this journey. It's how we heal, period.

I don't have all the answers but what I often turn to is a somatic approach to grief. But before we go there, let's look at the most widely accepted grief process, wherein there are five stages we all go through: denial/isolation, anger, bargaining, depression, and acceptance. According to grief experts. you can experience at least one or all of these phases at one time.

So what does that look like along the path of antiracism? Let's take a look:

It's a beautiful summer day, and you just happen to have the day off work. You're watching the local news and you hear "This just in, the police have concluded a high-speed chase. A woman, identified as Black, was running from the scene and has been shot by police."

Not paying any attention to it, you go about your day, thinking, *There's nothing I can do about that.*

An hour later a friend calls and says, "Have you seen the news?"

You reply, "What news?"

"You know," your friend insists, "about the Black girl."

You begin to speak, but before the words get out, your friend says, "Turn on BNN."

To your dismay, you see the full body-cam video of police chasing what appears to be a young girl down the street. The girl stops to turn around and begins to put her hands up. To your dismay, three shots ring out and the girl falls on the ground. You then see the officer walk over to the girl, check her pulse, and say an expletive. Afterward the news anchor comes back to the screen and makes a call to action for police accountability.

Tears begin to stream from your eyes. You get back on the phone with a friend and say, "Something has to be done about this. I cannot believe this happened."

Days go by after the event and the shock starts to subside and transform into anger. You see a local community protest and decide to join in, letting anger be your guide to moving forward. The anger turns into sleepless nights of phone calls to the local police department and anger at your family's lack of empathy for the situation. You continue on the path only to be met with depression that sends you spiraling into defeat. You begin to discredit yourself and the world we live in. Sleepless nights turn into days of calling off work because the world around you feels so heavy that there's no way to move forward. You feel alone and isolated as if there's no hope. Eventually you burn out from all the work you've been doing. You've disassociated from life and distanced yourself from everyone or anything that is a reminder of the injustice of the world. Eventually you move into acceptance.

Instead, you begin to educate yourself to learn and understand the weight of the world around you. You recognize that violence on Black bodies is a symptom of a bigger issue, and while you can't solve it overnight, you can work toward a liberated future. So you choose to let go of the people, places, or things that don't support your journey toward self- and collective liberation. You begin to accept you cannot change the system, but you can take responsibility for the harm you have caused in perpetuating it.

But in order to move through any of these actions, you must embrace grief, because not only are these the stages for grief, grief is the catalyst through the stages. Denial/isolation, anger, bargaining, depression, and acceptance will all be meaningless unless they are rooted in a deep sense of loss—for the life that you watched be so casually extinguished on TV, for the worldview that has offered you the life you are now living, for the people in that world who also continue to perpetuate the harm, either by ignoring it themselves or by intentionally participating in it. You are not broken, and there is nothing to fix, but grief is what propels us forward into growth and healing.

You might be saying, *Myisha, I hear you, but how do I know that I am actually grieving?* The goal here is not to stay stagnant in your grief but to move with it, as it will be ongoing in the work that we do. Because every moment a Black body is killed by police, you will grieve. Every moment an Asian elder is violated, you will grieve. Grief isn't taboo, it's a part of life. This is why my ancestors ritualize grief as an ongoing process. You know you're grieving by feeling the sensation in your body, when a topic creates an energetic charge that compels you to do something. You know you are moving with grief when you constantly worry about doing this work wrong, but you feel your fears and do the work anyway. Grief is actually not the never-ending loop of educator content, podcasts, books, and pamphlets on antiracism. They're an important part of the work, but they're only there for your intellect.

True co-conspiratorial work happens in the heart, and grief is the language of our hearts. Give it space to cry, to scream, to get you moving and working and staying committed no matter what losses might stand in our future—and there will be losses. Allow your tears to heal your way forward.

REFLECTION QUESTIONS ON
WHITE TEARS

· · · · · ·

1. Do you know how to connect with grief or do you push it down and keep it moving? Where did you learn to disconnect from grief? How will space to grieve allow you to heal on your antiracism journey?

2. When was the last time you took time to grieve your journey? Do you have a grief ritual? If not, what rituals do you need to create for your antiracism journey?

3. How will you keep yourself aware enough to know when you are weaponizing your tears?

· 4 ·

RADICAL LISTENING

"Listening is the most difficult skill to learn and the
most important to have."
—African proverb

As a co-conspirator, listening—especially radical listening—is a critical key on this journey. Through radical listening, we develop a practice of taking in information to help us better understand the things of which we are not aware. The goal of radical listening is to develop stronger interdependent relationships; it is how to become of better service to the world. In justice work, another reason we listen is to empathize with others in order to build relational communities, engaging in dialogue to help us understand complex issues.

In the marketing world, social listening is how brands track their social media platforms for conversations about their company and products. In racial justice work, I define social listening as the practice of listening to voices outside the eyes of whiteness. It's an intersectional approach to listen not only to scholars but also to folx on the ground across Black, Brown, AAPI,

LGBTQ+, and other marginalized spectrums. Social listening is a practice to understand what voices of color outside the binary are teaching and living.

After the murder of George Floyd, many well-meaning white people, maybe even you, participated in the #AmplifyMelanated-Voices challenge. The goal of the challenge was to amplify Black and Brown voices in the social justice movement. What was meant to be a radical moment of listening turned out to be just another performative act. White influencers utilized their platforms to elevate voices of those deemed "socially acceptable," "palatable," and "safe." The voices that mattered—activists on the ground, educators, the true mothers of the movement—were coincidentally left out of the conversation.

Those who were elevated gave their guidance across these white platforms while many white allies "listened" for that moment, before eventually dropping out of the movement. One's proximity to whiteness allows them to be able to say, "I'm not experiencing racism on the day to day so I can go back to whatever routine I had before." In fact, the closer you are to whiteness, the easier it is to avoid the void that can come after the perpetrations of nonwhite people and communities. We are conditioned by the neurological and chemical advances in our brain, which work actively all day to help us avoid the experience of pain. Our bodies also work on a spectrum—identifying pain as a precursor to death. So it's no surprise that the minute the work gets hard or hurtful, people choose to avoid it. They are hardwired to do so. But that is the whole goal of this work—to reprogram the hardwiring of our brains. To create a new neural pathway of how we understand, negotiate, and engage with the world.

But in order to reprogram our brains, we must
first start listening to a new program.

Radical listening is a skill that is learned and not necessarily acquired. Part of the journey toward a better understanding includes listening to voices that are in close proximity or have lived experience with institutional, structural, and interpersonal oppression. The goal is not to listen with the intention to fix or rescue someone, rather the goal is to understand the calling of their hearts, and the work you are now called to do. In order to begin to engage your own listening skills, think about how you have been impacted when someone listened deeply to you:

When was the last time you felt listened to?

Who were you talking to?

Where were you?

What were you talking about?

Did you feel seen, comforted, or validated or did you feel like the person pathologized your pain and didn't really listen?

Were they there to fix you or to understand you?

Because guess what, you can't do both at the same time. As a society, we've learned to listen to solve problems, giving our two cents as a form of rescuing folx from their own stories. Unconsciously we all operate as fixers because fixing gives us something to do—it provides us with the opportunity to play hero. But then guess who the focus moves to? When you watch a movie like

Black Panther, are you watching Chadwick Boseman (Rest in Power) or the people he just saved from harm? Patriarchy (and especially Christian patriarchy) has trained us to focus on the savior and not the saved. That's why when children speak their radical truth, we punish them for speaking, rather than listening to the gifts of their intelligence. Children are not allowed to save the day; they are only there to be saved. They are considered lambs of the flock but never the shepherd.

Like most parents, I was socialized with the belief that children should be seen and not heard. It was ingrained in me through church and the environment around me. My thoughts or opinions did not matter, and I was raised to treat my children the same way. Only thing is, my eleven-year-old son, Melech, is a great "truth teller." He has an innate ability to say it like it is even if it's uncomfortable.

One day he started with his truth telling from the back seat of the car. He had only said, "Mom, listen," when I felt an energetic charge in my body and quickly responded, "Melech, I'm the adult, you're the child, and you don't pay the bills here. So shut your mouth."

I looked at his face in the rearview mirror. He had dropped his head, his eyes were sullen, and it hit me: I had just told him his perspective didn't matter, violently forcing that truth on him with my "Shut up!"

I saw the centuries before me that conditioned this behavior, especially in Black families where parents feared that if their children weren't silent and perfect they could be removed at any time. And it isn't even just a historical fear, because whether it's CPS or law enforcement or the legacy of slavery, there is always a threat to Black parents over the fate of their children.

But in that moment, I recognized that I didn't want to raise my son under the fear of the oppressor; my job was to listen to his truth, even if I did not like it. My job was not to cut him off using the same patriarchal messaging I received in my youth. I did not need to fix what he was saying, and certainly not silence it, but rather reflect back to him so that he could hear himself. It is in giving him the opportunity to hear himself that he could be seen and known.

My mother often calls this "New Age" parenting. I like to think this is the parenting that honors humanity, and as hard as it is to practice, we gotta remember that our children are our mirrors. The reality is, I didn't have to agree with what his truth was, but giving him the space to speak his was a radical act of love—and, ultimately, an act of revolution against the fear that if they say the wrong thing, they might be harmed. Because if they can't share their hurt with their mothers, then they will need to share it somewhere else. I recognize I am the safest container for my children's hurt, anger, sadness, and confusion. It may be uncomfortable to listen, but the best lessons come when we learn to listen to the radical honesty of our children.

Our children are not the lambs, they are the shepherds, and if we allow ourselves to be guided by their wisdom, we find we are also guided back to our own mirrored truths.

In the book *Listen Like You Mean It,* author Ximena Vengoechea reminds us that:

> Most of us listen well enough, but without deliberate attention we may move through conversation with significant blind spots. It's easy for us to learn only part of the story, or

misunderstand it entirely. Miscommunication can escalate a neutral situation to a negative one, and make an already negative scenario worse.

We listen with the subconscious belief that we are in control of a narrative, that once we hear a story, we can then fix an issue. Which is why so many of us use listening as a self-serving tool to rescue someone versus making space for the true message that the speaker is trying to convey. We listen to prove we are right and confirm that our biases are true.

When we listen to fix anything, we fall back into a savior trope, which is a dangerous place to be for you as a white or white-passing person. The white savior is described as the white protagonist who fights to save a nondominant person or group from oppressive systems, thinking they are redeeming them. We see white saviorism everywhere—from movies to music videos, from social workers to school yards.

I can't even count how many well-meaning white mothers were proving their white virtue when they assumed that I could not speak up for myself or my children. When my daughter was in first grade another student told her that she couldn't come to his birthday party. In fact he said, "People with your skin color aren't invited to my house." Imagine the rage I felt at that moment when another child from a marginalized background said my daughter is uninvited. I went to speak with another mom, a well-meaning white woman, and she became hypervigilant.

"Myisha, what do you want me to do?" She immediately jumped into action. "That's inappropriate, we should go talk to the teacher."

A true co-conspirator asks, "What do you need in this situation? What does support look like for you?" But this was just another reminder that most white and white-passing people are looking to respond to pain, not understand it. They are not listening to reflect, but rather to rescue or fix it.

The goal is simple: You must learn how to listen in order to understand, *period*. And when we listen to understand, we minimize the need to fix anyone outside ourselves.

Most folx don't understand that listening is a process. We all have different listening skills and listening styles. The process of listening begins with receiving, interpreting, recalling, evaluating, and responding. At that first moment of listening, we receive a message. From there, we often interpret the information, recalling what we hear and evaluating what we believe to be the truth in the story. The danger in interpreting other people's experiences is that once you're done listening to the story, your brain can trick you into creating scenarios of what an individual may or may not need based on your evaluation of their circumstances. This is why it's important to understand what listening is and what *your* listening style is.

It's also important to note that the listening process doesn't have a definite start or finishing point. We know that our brains can hold large amounts of information for a long period of time. According to the book *Making Conflict Suck Less*, "Sensory storage is very large in terms of capacity but limited in terms of length of storage. We can hold large amounts of unsorted visual information but only for about a tenth of a second. By comparison, we can hold large amounts of unsorted auditory information for longer— up to four seconds."[1]

When we break down the process of listening, we can slowly begin to see our own blind spots when it comes to how we hear and interpret the world. It is also important to recognize the different types of listening and listening styles, which include the discriminative, informational, critical, and empathic. In the work of co-conspiratorship, the goal is to engage in all four types of listening. When you are on a social media livestream, participating in a workshop, or listening to a podcast, you are moving through informational and discriminative listening. You're receiving information, processing, and deciphering how to utilize it for your journey. You are critically listening when you are taking in information and critiquing what you know is true on the journey ahead.[2] Lastly, you are empathic listening when you are working to understand and feel where the speaker is coming from. For example, when someone asks, "Do you feel me?" and you actually do, connecting not just into their words, or your intellectual understanding of them, but into their lived emotional experience, where you do indeed "feel them," that means you're empathically receiving and connecting to the message that is being shared with you. Empathic listening is also key for the connection and community building necessary for this work.

DO NOW: Write. Take a few minutes to journal and reflect on the following prompt: What is this information inviting me to know or do?

In addition to the different types of listening, there are also four distinct listening styles: people-oriented, action-oriented, content-oriented, and time-oriented listening. Each listening style serves a whole purpose, however in justice work, you should be flowing and rotating in all four types of listening to help you be in a state of action. Listening to the people's needs through different content mediums will help you build the time management and resilience skills to be in the action of antiracism work. In order to gauge how to flow through the listening process, you will need to understand your distinct listening style. Two people can hear the same message, but the context will be understood differently depending on the individual's style.

When I was once part of a listening project, one of the key things I learned was the importance of empathic listening and reflection. I'll never forget the moment that I was out listening in Oakland. I had a genuine and sweet conversation with a man I met about his life. After spending time together he said, "Wow, it really feels good to be listened to. I'm usually the one listening to everyone else's problems. It feels good to hear for myself. Thank you."

I was blown away by the fact that just by listening with empathy, compassion, and understanding, someone could finally have the opportunity to hear themselves, to hear their own truth. This is what gets lost when we rush in to fix someone else's problem. They don't have the opportunity to experience their own truth of a situation because the truth gets hijacked by the savior.

On your journey to becoming a co-conspirator, you begin to learn it's not about you or your perceptions, it's about hearing from voices that matter, and then moving closer into proximity of their truth, not your evaluation of their story.

Radical listening is hard because our brains are always working to filter, process, and interpret information, which in turn affects our decisions and judgments. In one of my courses, "Breaking Up with Bias," I utilize what is known as the bias codex to help folx understand how cognitive bias works and its relationship to the listening process. The cognitive bias codex is a graphic image with over 180 cognitive biases or blind spots around which our brains are conditioned to confirm our beliefs. The thing about bias is that we don't recognize it's happening until it's pointed out to us.

Cognitive biases are filtered through four domains of processing: too much information, the need to act fast, what we should remember, and not enough meaning. When we are listening, we are always filtering out information from the four processing areas. For example, when you think you are open and listening to a BIPOC educator, you may be processing the information from the lens of confirmation bias. When listening for urgency, you might not make appropriate time for reflection, integration, or healing. During the 2021 terrorist attack on the Capitol, many were listening and moving from urgency rather than recalling the previous information they had learned along their antiracism journey.

On that day, many white and white-passing people believed they were the exception to the rule, which only leads to the dangerous upholding of interlocking systems of oppression. Because no matter how many conversations, trainings, and podcasts people have listened to, many were far too worried about being a good white person than listening to the marginalized voices calling you in. You may have been listening but your own cognitive bias, need to act fast, or uncertainty as to what to remember blocked your ability to decenter whiteness. Even those who were convinced that they were decentering whiteness began flooding educators' inboxes asking what to do. But if you had truly been listening, you would have already known.

The problem is that you haven't truly learned to empathetically listen to Black voices because you have been conditioned your whole life to think that if it ain't white, it ain't right.

If a white educator told you what to do, it would stick like glue because we are socialized to see whiteness as the representation of virtue. Historically, whiteness has always created the narratives and told the stories. We are just now getting to a place where marginalized people are the center of the stories and your cognitive blind spots don't know how to make the connection. If you spend most your life watching mass media and seeing how marginalized folx are portrayed, whether you want to admit it or not, you might be listening in the front row, but in the back, you are still running with the biases you were socialized to see.

According to bell hooks, "Popular culture creates and perpetuates sexist and racist thinking. Movies and media are lead propaganda machines to instill hegemonic order, and white supremacy frames a world that we all have a relationship to (framework and systems, not individuals). We are all in collusion through cultural and hegemonic order."

If you're used to only white voices being the voice of reason, it will influence how you listen to Black, Brown, Indigenous, Southeast Asian, Asian American, or Pacific Islander voices. You won't recognize your aversion to these voices until you move out of performative allyship and into co-conspiratorship. A co-conspirator needs to be constantly asking themselves, *Who am I listening to? What is the call to action they want me to respond to? Who is being helped and impacted by the work?* And most importantly, *How am I decentering whiteness as I am listening to voices in the movement?* Who you center and listen to matters.

Because if you are listening to and centering mostly white voices in this work, you're doing it wrong. As a white person, you have been socialized to expect comfort, credentials, and palatability—a soothing PhD with a side of chicken soup. The truth of the matter is whiteness rewards softness, conditioning us to seek warm, nurturing voices. White folx have created the context of the conversation and the binary. But intellectualization does not allow you to drop into yourself and truly understand or locate yourself in this space. In fact, quite the opposite. It gives you permission to be stuck, stay stuck, and ghost your antiracism journey. A good friend of mine, Louiza Doran says, "Whiteness cannot see outside itself."

Because here's the thing, if you were socialized to uphold whiteness, how can you possibly teach what you haven't lived? This is not to discredit the white folx who've gone to school studying race, critical race theory, and whiteness. But if someone white understands the practice of critical race theory, and history of whiteness, they would understand the importance of decentering themselves in the work.

Critical race theory (CRT), a term coined by legal scholar Kimberlé Crenshaw, "exposes the ways that racism is often cloaked in terminology regarding 'mainstream,' 'normal,' or 'traditional' values or 'neutral' policies, principles, or practices."[3] There are five tenets of critical race theory, which highlight the importance of decentering whiteness in the work, one of which offers, "Recognition of the relevance of people's everyday lives to scholarship. This includes embracing the lived experiences of people of color, including those preserved through storytelling, and rejecting deficit-informed research that excludes the epistemologies of people of color."

In a nutshell, CRT is about embracing the lived experience of people of color and the ways in which we share, teach, and preserve our information. Historically, white folx have written all the stories and created the narrative of whiteness. Due to colonization, exploitation, and racial socialization, white folx, and especially white men, are the experts in exerting authoritative power and colonization. It was white men who created the construct of race. It was white men who wrote the journals and notes to describe enslaved Africans as brutes and Indigenous peoples as savages. It was the written word of white men that created the single story of truth and white women who co-conspired with them to uphold it. Don't forget 40 percent of slave owners were white women. According to Chimamanda Adichie, if we hear only a single story about another person or country, we risk a critical misunderstanding.

If you only hear a single narrative reinforcing white normalcy, it increases your biases, which are already shaped by media, community, and industry.

And as a white person, if you are listening only to other white people, it gives you permission to stay within the binary, not only reinforcing cognitive bias but white comfort. It keeps you from really feeling or sitting with yourself. This is why white people struggle to sit with emotions, and often dismiss the emotions they learn along the journey. Co-conspirators describe this as the ability to step in at a surface level but then return to suppressing emotions and thoughts. It was shared by my co-conspirator participant Anne Mendel that, "We white people can use tools like therapy to heal and change, but we forget that even in therapy it gives us a pass and we still uphold the system. It helps us all adjust better to staying in the system, not pushing away from it. Essentially even in a therapeutic setting, we are still being socialized to stay complicit."

As someone who has benefitted from culturally competent therapy and holds peer support groups, I am in no way demeaning therapy. But we also have to remember that therapy was created by white men to support white middle-class folx from experiencing "abnormal" mental deficiencies. Remember anything that is seen as "abnormal or inferior" is obscure and unacceptable to the white lens. So for white people in a white therapeutic setting, you're getting help and it feels intellectually good, but unless it is also culturally competent, your therapist can still be socializing you to uphold the system. If a therapist is giving you only tools that intellectually stimulate but disconnect you from the head and heart of your journey, you are only being further disconnected from embodied connection.

This is where listening to marginalized voices can come into play.

LISTENING TO MARGINALIZED VOICES

One of my elders once told me, "White people listen to you because you're good at white speaking. You have a natural teacher's voice, so you make them feel comfortable. I can't speak to white people; they see me as a threat because I don't have that teacher voice like you."

What this elder is inviting me to know is that whiteness expects palatability, and because I grew up around white people and was at one point socialized white in Black skin, I am not seen as a threat to most white people.

As a white person, you've probably never noticed your reaction when listening to marginalized voices. You haven't realized that you shy away from voices that aren't palatable to you. You don't recognize that you have been trained to see nonwhite voices as threatening. You haven't been willing to admit that voices that don't speak proper English, pronounce words correctly, or uphold "the king's English" make you shy away from supporting marginalized peoples. Tone and diction are key components to listening. If you hear a tone that isn't satisfying, you will naturally avoid it. But instead of ignoring voices that make you move away, the invitation is to ask yourself these questions: *What about this individual is making me uncomfortable? What is this inviting me to know or do? How can I lean into my aversion instead of running away from it?*

You have to be willing to get to the root of your aversion, otherwise you will stay above the soil of your journey. Listening to marginalized voices is a deep practice of dropping below the surface of that soil, connecting into the rooted intuition from which so much of whiteness works to disconnect us. Intuition and somatic work have a lot to do with this journey, but so does listening.

Most white folx's relationships are rooted at a surface level. When listening, you're listening for a quick fix or a quick answer, but you're never really listening somatically, in a way where you can actually feel yourself. One co-conspirator shared:

> My family is very much surface; they can't talk about much beyond the weather, right? But for some people, I've been able to chip past that when there's a theme of this desire of wanting more, but not even knowing what that is. And so, I think there's dissatisfaction with the surface, but not an understanding about what I am talking about, with the head and the heart and the in and the out being the same. Listening to you and other marginalized voices helps me get to the root of myself and the somatic experience associated with that.

When we listen to marginalized voices, we not only have the opportunity to learn more, but to integrate those lessons into the head, heart, and hands of the journey forward.

EMPATHY, NVC, AND RADICAL LISTENING

We are not trained to listen with empathy, communicate nonviolently, or hold space for one another. Empathic listening is a practice that allows you to reflect what is being said, by seeing yourself in someone else's shoes. It allows you to develop intellectual understanding and emotional connection with someone outside of yourself. Empathy is required when listening to voices of the global majority—not sympathy and not apathy. We need a bold empathy to hold space for our voices and to move the future from the violence of the past and the passivity of the present into future action.

According to the Center for Nonviolent Communication, "Nonviolent communication (NVC) is based on the principles of nonviolence—the natural state of compassion when no violence is present in the heart. NVC begins by assuming that we are all compassionate by nature and that violent strategies—whether verbal or physical—are learned behaviors taught and supported by the prevailing culture."

Nonviolent communication was first practiced and utilized by Mahatma Gandhi, followed by Martin Luther King Jr., and normalized into white culture by Dr. Marshall Rosenberg. Gandhi saw violence as passive and physical. According to him, "Passive violence is a daily affair, consciously and unconsciously. It is the fuel that ignites the fire of physical violence." Gandhi understood violence from its Sanskrit root *himsa,* meaning injury. Instead, he utilized the concept of *ahisma* to "do no harm" in his social and political protest. As Gandhi explained, "Ahimsa is the highest duty. Even if we cannot practice it in full, we must try to understand its spirit and refrain as far as is humanly possible from violence."[4] Dr. Martin Luther King Jr. adopted Gandhi's principle of ahisma. Dr. King believed that "the Christian doctrine of love operating through the Gandhian method of nonviolence was one of the most potent weapons available to oppressed people in their struggle for freedom."[5]

Dr. Marshall Rosenberg, known to give reverence to Gandhi and MLK for their work in the movement, formalized a process of inquiry to help couples and individuals communicate nonviolently. For most folx, this practice or process isn't a normal way of being, as it involves a conscious awareness of one's observations, feelings, needs, and requests. When listening to voices of the global majority, I encourage you to utilize the NVC approach to listening—not listening to respond, but accepting what you hear as an invitation to learn, grow, and be in conscious community.

When we spend time understanding and knowing how to listen, we cultivate better relationships. Oftentimes, relationships fail due to poor listening and lack of self-awareness in the process. When you are blindly listening, you miss the opportunity to learn from the perspective of someone else. Most times we are listening to fix others, attempting to take in the information to solidify our own understanding. When you are listening to fix someone, then you're moving into saviorism or rescuing behavior. Everyone wants to be the hero in someone else's story. Listening with compassion and empathy allows you to be your own hero along *your* healing journey. It is important to remember that people are not broken, and when we see folx as whole human beings, we are able to listen from a space of nonviolence and compassion.

REFLECTION QUESTIONS ON RADICAL LISTENING

· · · · · ·

I've created a few prompts to help you get to the root of your listening.

1. Who am I listening to? Why? What's in it for me?

2. Listening to marginalized voices is the invitation to interrogate your aversion.

3. What about this individual is making me uncomfortable? What is this inviting me to know or do? How can I lean into aversion instead of running away from it?

4. Audit your social feeds.

5. Take a few minutes to audit who you are listening to on your journey.

6. What are they inviting you to know or do?

7. How are they helping your progress?

8. What do you want to learn more about? Does your feed reflect your values?

9. Practice NVC to listen well to marginalized voices.

· 5 ·

LIFELONG LEARNING

"Real learning comes about when the
competitive spirit has ceased."
—Jiddu Krishnamurti

I can count on my fingers and toes the number of times I was told as a youth that school was all I needed to survive in this world. I was told that, as a Black woman, if I went after the American dream by taking the pathway to college and career, I would be able to meet the same standards of living as my white counterparts. What we didn't realize about the myth of the American dream was how insidious systemic oppression would be, limiting the access of those who had a marginalized identity.

Traditional schooling, or ways of learning, does not prepare folx who hold a marginalized identity for the levels of microaggression, barriers to promotion and raises, as well as the systemic injustices and pay gaps faced by American workers every day. Traditional modes of schooling do not invite embodied and restorative response to pain and trauma. Instead, it punishes those who hold a marginalized identity and who can't sit in a classroom. In the United States, traditional ways of learning are all about mastery, but when we think about it, we are being asked to master the interlocking systems of oppression. We're socialized to do as the system says and as it does, and the moment that we decide to take a break from the traditional ways of being, we get punished.

As a child, I could not stand being in traditional classroom settings. There was just something awkward and unnatural about being forced to be still all day long. Sitting inside an enclosed building and being served hot meals, while having knowledge shoved down my throat was not life-giving or easy. All of us in a traditional classroom were being socialized to master a task, or we'd be seen as failures. We were also being forced to pledge allegiance every day to a country that was brutalizing Black folx on a daily basis.

I will never forget my third-grade teacher, Mrs. Parquet. She followed the rules of assimilation to a T, so much so that she ran her classroom like a military boot camp. We had very strict behavioral expectations set for us. For example, if we didn't stand up during the Pledge of Allegiance, it was an automatic call home and we were sent to the office for noncompliance. I couldn't stand going to her classroom and sitting all day waiting for the bell to ring for recess, lunch, and PE. It was a nightmare; even thinking through this experience reminds me that school was not created for us to be lifelong learners. In fact, school was designed to shut down the imagination and our curiosity for learning.

Learning in school is about mastery, and mastery in education looks different depending on where you went to school and the socioeconomic status of the community and school district. Mastery learning requires that students attain a given level in order to move forward. The problem with this is offering students enough time to learn in order to reach the same level of learning. Mastery learning is an ableist approach to education, denying us that we are all different and that our learning styles must be met in order for us to refine what we know. It socialized us to believe that if we don't get it, we just aren't good enough. And in turn, it built a generation of adults who see themselves as different, inferior, or not good enough. Because the classrooms weren't created for social and emotional growth, they were designed for peer-to-peer competition. Which is why many of us see education as a competition to be won, not a tool to shift our perspectives. It was in school that we learned the importance of citizenship, perfect attendance, and being the teacher's pet. The US education system is not interested in growth over time. Instead, it reinforces supremacy in a way that rewards the good girl/good boy trope and demonizes kids who "act out" due to a lack of necessary stimulation or overstimulation.

GENERATIVE LEARNING

Many individuals close to my age (high-end millennials) struggled to meet mastery criteria and instead were moved into special education classrooms, held back a grade, or were labeled as "troubled students" if we didn't keep up with our peers. Mastery does not allow space for refining as we go or generative learning. According to Merlin C. Wittrock, "Generative learning is, therefore, the process of constructing meaning through generating relationships and associations between stimuli and existing knowledge, beliefs, and experiences."

Generative learning doesn't place individuals in a box, or force them to compete in order to be seen or valued. Instead, it makes space for the lifelong learning necessary to grow and change over time; it offers us the opportunity to experience our humanity on this journey of life. Even on one's antiracism journey, we largely ignore generative learning because performance-based learning and metrics are seen as valued, instead of as constructs that need to be dismantled.

I don't know when your great awakening began but one thing I know is that it likely triggered a feeling of panic. As a white person, you may have been living your everyday life and then realized, *Holy shit, I've got a lot to learn.* That holy-shit moment can take you down the path of thinking, *I need to be a good white person.*

The notion of a good white person is rooted in the binary, choosing one version or the other, versus both/and. Panic pushes us to perform rather than to drop into acceptance and the process of practice.

The notion of being a better white person essentially takes you on a path of *How do I master not being racist so I don't show up the wrong way?* Essentially your wake-up drove you into a state of flight, fight, or freeze. From there, you probably quite naturally rushed in, deciding that you must learn the way you have always mastered a topic, not slowing down to really understand, integrate, and know what modes of learning work best for you. The problem with panic as a motivator is that it moves us into the urgency of trying to figure out where to begin, what book to read first, whose container to join, and how to make sure you get it right the first time. We have been trained through centuries of oppression to believe that we must get things right the first time, because errors in work cost time and money, shaming us to believe that a mistake means we are totally flawed. But mistakes just mean we are learning.

DO NOW: Take a walking meditation. If you've been reading for at least fifteen minutes, take time to connect to your body. Walking meditation is a Buddhist practice that allows us to mindfully connect with ourselves. The Greater Good Science Center in Berkeley shares the following practice to walk and meditate: Walk ten to fifteen steps along the lane you've chosen and then pause and breathe for as long as you like. When you're ready, turn and walk back in the opposite direction to the other end of the lane, where you can pause and breathe again. Then, when you're ready, turn once more and continue with the walk.

The traditional education system has us wrestling to master multiple subjects at the same time, pushing us to get it done, by any means necessary, so that we can tick a box and consider our task complete. But this journey is not about ticking a box. This journey is going to require you to integrate lifelong learning by understanding your learning style, what you need to know, and how it is through failing your way forward that you move ahead. The goal of becoming actively antiracist is not mastery, it is about refining what you know over time to learn to be a better person (not necessarily a good white person). Being a co-conspirator can feel isolating, overwhelming, and confusing. At any given moment you might feel like you aren't doing enough, but it is in this unknowing that we begin to understand. It is in the slowness and frustration of the process that we actually have the chance to embody our learning, instead of simply memorizing it and moving on.

I remember teaching a workshop in the Bay Area where most of the participants were cisgender white women and one man. During a group breakout, the white man pulled me to the side and asked, "Why aren't you as aggressive as XYZ educator?"

At that moment I was shocked by the "caucacity" of this white man. He came to learn and yet, he dared to take up space by asking that question.

Rather than respond, I became curious and asked him, "What makes you think it's appropriate to ask me that question?"

After a moment of silence and reflection, the man said, "Well, based on my experience with *that* Black woman, I assumed that you all were aggressive. I see aggression as a powerful tool for women, especially Black women."

At that moment, I asked a co-conspirator to take over the conversation so that I could regulate myself. I excused myself from the space and while collecting myself, I had to breathe into my feelings. I felt the hairs stand up on my arms, and a cold frustration and overwhelm flooded my body. Upon reflection it was clear to me that I was not the teacher for him, not because I was a Black woman, but because his own bias and ignorance of Black women meant I couldn't meet his learning style. I could have allowed that experience to break me, but instead I recognized that his learning style was from a teacher who replicated domination and patriarchy, not someone like myself who leaned into the duality of matriarchy and patriarchy.

REQUIREMENTS FOR LIFELONG LEARNING

Lifelong learning requires you to slow down enough to recognize your learning style and the ways in which you process information. Lifelong learning is remembering you have choices around how you learn, who you learn from, and knowing what teaching styles work best for you. This isn't me saying to prioritize your needs over folx within a marginalized community. What I am suggesting is that not all teachers help you "get it." The learning process is a multisensory experience that begins when you break up with socialized learning and mastery and instead, cultivate knowledge on what helps you grow. Not all plants need the same fertilizer or food, but nourishment is what keeps the plants' growth sustainable. If antiracism work is a practice or embodiment, we must figure out our ways of knowing, learning, and practicing. Learning isn't just about what you know, it's also about how you feel and what you do.

One of the paths to pursuing lifelong learning is understanding that as a co-conspirator an individual educational plan (IEP) is required to commit to the process. In a traditional educational setting, an IEP is a legal document that is developed for each public school child in the United States who needs special education. It is created through a team of the child's parent and district personnel who are knowledgeable about the child's needs. As a mother of miracles, I've spent many years advocating for IEPs for all my children. Advocacy is a tough job, and I am using the IEP as a clear path to help folx understand the learning process. There isn't a one-size-fits-all approach to learning. In fact, it requires you to know yourself, your processing style, and how you recall information. Currently, educators have identified seven distinct learning styles that can help you understand how you take in, process, practice, and retain information.

They are verbal, visual, auditory, physical/tactile, logical, solitary, and social. A verbal learner prefers learning via speech and writing. If this style of learning works for you, you may need captions, recordings, and role-playing scenarios to help you process information. A visual learner prefers pictures and images to take in information. If this is your style of learning, you may notice your need for mind maps, patterns, colors, or stimulating visuals to help you take in information. If you attend a workshop and find yourself understimulated and bored because there are no slides, it might be that your learning style isn't being met.

An auditory learner appreciates sound, rhyme, and music to help them remember what's important. If this feels familiar, you may be someone who desires rhythm, sound recordings, or background music to help you learn. In some workshops, I find co-conspirators who make rhymes out of the content. I recognized rhymes help them remember and recall information faster. A physical learner prefers to learn with their body, hands, or sense of touch. Some co-conspirators I've worked with have used this style of learning, and have painted, cooked, or used gentle movement during workshops to learn this way. A logical learner prefers reasoning, logic, and systems to comprehend. If this sounds familiar, you probably pick up systems and processes easily. You also work to understand the reasons behind the work you produce. Most logical co-conspirators I work with call themselves overthinkers, as they struggle to make the next move until the current move is all figured out.

A solitary learner prefers to work alone and self-study. This may be you if you get overwhelmed working in a group setting. You may see the community as a huge distraction whereas social learners benefit by learning in groups or communities. A social learner is driven by working with others as much as possible, while practicing how to be interdependent in community. Most social learners are seeking human connection, so their work or commitments don't feel isolated or alone. They see community as a gift and not as a curse.

> Social learners who are co-conspirators aren't looking to fix or rescue folx; they are individuals who are striving to show up for others and themselves.

While many of us may have a favorable or prominent style of learning, one style of learning that I haven't mentioned is what I like to call combination or integration. The integration of learning is a sensory somatic experience that can help individuals thrive in their learning containers. It is an integrative learning style connecting the head with visual and auditory processing in order to take in knowledge. It also connects to the heart, which requires you to get into movement and action with your hands. Engaging in work that allows you to tap into the senses is work that allows you to lean into your discomfort and regulate. And a learning environment that allows you to engage the senses is one that supports social emotional learning (SEL).

When my children were a part of the Oakland Unified School District, the district implemented SEL as a process to help students develop self-awareness, self-control, and interpersonal skills. Teachers in the elementary school setting walked around with necklaces that reminded students of the importance of empathy, respect, mindfulness, decision-making, and self-awareness. I remember seeing the necklaces and telling myself, *If they made something similar for me as a child, I probably would have become a better-regulated adult.* This is not suggesting that school practices are always (or often) used at home, but the awareness of such practices can help families make the curiosity of learning more enjoyable.

It is said that folx who have strong social-emotional skills are better able to cope with everyday challenges and benefit academically, professionally, and socially. Most of us high-end millennials did not know about SEL or a sensory-based approach to learning. This is why most of us are easily dysregulated in learning containers because we don't know how to process information that triggers us, disconnecting us from feeling our senses.

> **As a white person, you need to engage in the senses in order to navigate the experience of waking up to whiteness.**

Integration means that you will access the parts of your sensory system that are holding on to the trauma associated with learning. In most antiracism trainings, white folx are being taught at, not guided through a sensory practice. In our Co-Conspirators Lounge for instance, we begin with a welcoming ritual, community connection, and mindfulness practices. We continue the social sensory process by incorporating movement when necessary. Our first agreement in our learning spaces is for folx to be their most liberated selves. This requirement means people need to know what tools allow them to sit through a training, engage, and not intellectualize the process. I often tell folx, "If you need to dance, paint, bounce, cook, do what you need to sit in this space and be deep in your senses today."

It's almost taboo to hold space that engages the system, but in order to learn integration, you must practice integration. I also know that integration isn't for everyone. Folx who are introverts may not necessarily embrace or even need a sensory-based approach to do this work, and that's okay. Most folx who know their learning style is solitary create what works best for them. This is the power of the work, the power to adapt your learning style to what works best for you.

White traditional education forces mastery, but when you step into this life journey, it is not about mastery but practice. As famed pedagogue and author Paulo Freire writes, "Education is a matter of politics as well as pedagogy. The practice of education for liberation takes place in circumstances of specific power relations. Fundamental expression is given to power and politics and reflected in the meaning of language. Liberatory pedagogy incorporates a struggle for meaning as well as a struggle for freedom and justice."

The practice of becoming antiracist is like exercising a muscle. There is no graduation, merely a more powerful strength built over time. Liberatory learning offers that constant and ongoing improvement by offering you the grace to learn in a way that works for you, honors your humanity, and deepens the call into the work you're doing.

LIBERATORY LEARNING

Your antiracism journey should embody your learning style and be a liberatory experience. Liberation is the act of setting someone free from imprisonment, slavery, or oppression; it is a release. Therefore, liberatory learning is the practice of critical thinking, self-actualization, and the humanism of this work. If liberation is the freedom of oppression, then you shouldn't allow yourself to be or feel oppressed in how you learn the work required on the journey ahead.

Liberatory pedagogy is a liberating, life-affirming, humanizing, and democratic pedagogy that strives to unveil the true nature of reality, i.e., truth.[1] It allows for the opportunity to get things wrong without the condemnation of self or others for "failing." Liberatory learning allows you to free yourself from the self and the world's limitations of this journey. You are allowed to ditch the overwhelm that takes you down the cycle of guilt and shame.

As a white person, liberating your relationship with learning invites you to practice presence. It is the idea of walking through the fire without running from it. Don't get it twisted; it may feel taboo to think that your humanity should be honored as you lean into this work. The reality is, if you're treated like you don't have rights, you are upholding your own oppression. Learning the work should be a liberatory experience. The practices of liberation and learning are not rooted in shame. In fact, it is shame that keeps us prisoner to the analysis paralysis that can plague our journey.

Many folx learning on this journey are stuck in the paralysis of shame. You overanalyze content and context and stay in the headiness of the work. This is why many of you struggle with taking action. You've become paralyzed from the awakening and aren't sure of the next right move. You lack the ability to empathize with your own fears and confusion because supremacy has taught you to shame yourself into silence.

When we can't accept we aren't experts, we get stuck in being the know-it-all.

Unfortunately, friend, you can't be the expert in something you don't experience, but what you can do is empathize, reflect, and move forward toward integration. You are spending more time focused on what you don't know than leaning into accepting that "you don't know anything." When you admit you don't know anything, you release control and expectations. Giving yourself permission to free your learning journey allows you to open yourself up to learning in a liberatory way.

NICHE DOWN YOUR JOURNEY: THE CO-CONSPIRATOR'S IEP

During a period of IG Lives, where white folx kept asking me, "What can I do?" the concept of "Niche Down Your Journey" began to flow through me. I remembered an old-school marketing concept of "niching down" to have focus on your marketing audience. I took that same idea and applied it to one's healing journey. It was my hope that the concept would help people focus forward with bite-size pieces. I created a journal to help people with this work, explaining to them that without focus, you will ghost the process before you get started. Many co-conspirators jump into this work overconsumed with content educators and resources. The idea of "niche down" is to help you not feel overwhelmed on your journey. The invitation is to slow down, reduce overconsumption, and trust yourself during the process.

Earlier, I mentioned the need for an Individual Education Plan (IEP), which includes the learner, the IEP team, present levels of performance, goals, services, and any additional supplementary services. As a mother who has gone through the IEP process over the last eleven years, I can tell you that this process is extremely overwhelming. I recall the multiple medical, mental, and educational assessments given to me and my son by the IEP team. The heartbreaking truth is that the team typically upheld district policies rooted in systemic oppression. There were times that I knew my child needed an IEP, and the districts told me the opposite. The IEP team's voice was larger than my own, and I was supposed to be a "member of the team."

The co-conspirator's IEP is rooted in oppressive policies, but it requires you to know your learning style and the application of niching down your journey, which was a process I created after the murder of George Floyd. Many of you signed up for multiple workshops, listened to multiple programs, and followed online accounts that educated you for free. With the overwhelming consumption of content, many of you found yourself overwhelmed with the process. What I know as a guide is that if you're involved in too many things, you will crash and burn. Without focus, you will ghost the process before you get started. Many co-conspirators jump into this work overconsumed by content educators and resources. The idea of "niche down" is to help you to not feel overwhelmed on your journey. The invitation is to slow down, reduce overconsumption, and trust yourself during the process.

Niching down is simple:

1. It starts with you knowing your learning style followed by breaking down your educational learning into four ninety-day periods.

2. In each of those periods of time, you commit to engage deeply with one educator, guide, or scholar. Commit to reading one book, noticing, and notating along the way.

3. Next you'll support one local nonprofit, financially or with your talents and time.

4. Lastly, you will practice your journey one hour a day throughout your week to ensure the sustainability of your work. Essentially this practice allows you to learn in a liberatory way and eliminate the pressure of learning to master or perform.

Ultimately lifelong learning is driven by a deep desire for greater empathy, compassion, and understanding (of self, of others and of the complicated and nuanced world in which we exist). In my experience, the pain and discomfort of not pursuing lifelong learning is far greater than the pain and discomfort of learning (and unlearning) that is a constant part of lifelong learning. It is more than a mindset; it is a way of being. That is a constant part of it. It's a way of being and existing. Lifelong learning requires self-initiation, self-motivation, and an ongoing commitment to self, i.e., *I am not doing it for anybody else.* The power of stepping into lifelong learning is liberating and requires a deliberate and necessary ongoing practice. If you've ever played a sport or musical instrument, you know the dedication required to practice. A practice isn't perfect and the goal isn't perfection. Lifelong learning is a daily intentional awareness of informing yourself with what you need to know on your individual journey that helps support the collective of humanity. It's taking five minutes out of your day to communicate, read, listen, and share the nuances of your journey. It's practicing the commitment to yourself first to continue every day. And when you do, the paralyzing fear of failure will cease.

REFLECTION QUESTIONS ON LIFELONG LEARNING

· · · · · ·

1. Take a few moments and think about how you know what you know. Where did you first learn your name? How about your interests? Who taught you to read and write?

2. Reflecting on your answers, when did you decide for yourself how you wanted to read and write? What was this unlearning process like?

3. What is your learning style? Are you an auditory, visual, tactile learner? How can you use this information to determine your learning style?

4. Do you believe in mastery? If so, has this belief caused any hiccups in your life?

5. Think about liberators' learning. What comes to mind when you think of learning in a liberator way? Is it a reality or do you believe it is or can be a practice?

· 6 ·

ACTION IS NOT A PERFORMANCE

"All the world's a stage and all the men
and women merely players."

—William Shakespeare

According to mainstream media, 2020 fueled the largest social movement in American history. But I beg to differ because a social movement would have led to widespread resistance, institutional change, and a revolution in policy and philosophy. Nope, what we saw in 2020 through the middle of 2021 was actually just the greatest white performance in American history. Folx spent that time stuntin' the work and not living into it. *Stuntin'* is a Black term that means "pretending to be someone you aren't or pretending to have something you don't have." In the workplace and on the streets, most white folx showed up as allies out of convenience and fear, going through the three phases of white performance that many individuals first experience on this journey.

First, the Great White Awakening. Fueled by the publicized death of George Floyd, white folx began to wake up to the reality that something wasn't right. The awakening continued as more Black death dominated the news and the narrative for the rest of the summer. Black trauma fueled performative action by white allies and "antiracism" experts. We saw movements like "Black Out Tuesday," #AmplyfyMelanatedVoices, IG Takeovers, and more center experts like myself for a period of three to four months. But when Black death was no longer a spectacle, apathy began to set in and many folx's performances began to slow down. That is until The Great White Shock 'n' Awe. The January 6 terrorist attack on the Capitol caused the same folx who were awakened to violence against Black bodies to quickly "other" their white counterparts who weren't woke enough to be on the co-conspirators' journey.

This type of othering was seen in comments saying "those white people," "those Trump supporters" or even "THOTS." Yes, I saw comments using the Black vernacular term, "those hoes over there," to describe those other kinds of white folx who terrorized the nation's capital. A few weeks later, president-elect Joe Biden was inaugurated into office, and well, the Great White Ghosting began. I don't know why folx think President Biden is Captain Save-a-Ho, but what I do know is that many folx saw him as the Great White Savior who'd come in and rescue us from the policies of the Trump administration. By now, I hope most folx have realized . . . That. Was. A. Lie. The current administration is just the same package with a different bow. The problem is that between inherent white apathy, the COVID vaccinations, and the haphazard return to "normal," white folx have decided that they're cool to perform whenever and however they please, showing up for racial justice on demand and without consistency. Unfortunately, showing up on demand doesn't help in this work, as performing causes more harm than good.

ACTION IS NOT A PERFORMANCE

Real action is not a performance, but unfortunately, systemic oppression has trained and socialized us to believe that as long as it looks like we care, change will come.

Growing up, I was told that life is a stage and I am the main character. I believed that in this production, I got to choose the characters who would ultimately show up and play a role on my stage, but this notion offered me a false sense of self, leading me to believe that I could build my life by my own design.

Prior to Bill Cosby being exposed as a predator, *The Cosby Show* was proof that such a life was possible, helping me imagine the life I wanted to build, and the stage I strived to be seen on. The Huxtables were the epitome of Black excellence in white America. It felt surreal to me to see a couple who went to predominantly Black colleges get a piece of the American dream, raise six children, and send them to college. Yes, they faced issues, but they got through them together.

Their performances solidified them as Black brilliance in a "postracial world." The show, and its actors, reinforced the idea that Black people, including myself, could have it all. *The Cosby Show* promised Black folx that it would be a piece of cake to thrive, as long as we lived up to white cultural norms. In an imperialist, capitalist, white supremacist, patriarchal world, I would be seen as normal as long as I upheld the white constructs of success. My mom calls this "The American Dream."

My mother and her siblings were raised to go to school, get a degree, buy a home, and keep their head above water by staying silent, getting a check, retiring early, and striving to be seen as a good American person. I watched my mother work as a Black single mom, doing her best to give my brother and I our shot at

living the American dream by relocating us to Concord, California, from Chicago. But I never understood the costs of socializing
into whiteness until I realized the myth of the American dream,
which enforces one to uphold rugged individualism, all-
or-nothing thinking, competition between women (especially
Black women), the demonization of marginalized cultures, and
the glorification of Western Christianity.

Each of these tools is often used to oppress ourselves and the
collective. How many times have you been in a group situation
and there are unspoken rules of engagement? Recently a friend
of mine shared this: "This past weekend I spent some time hanging out with some of the other white kindergarten moms in my
daughter's class. The insecurity and pressure to conform and to
say all the right things runs so deep. Just the idea of vulnerability,
of sharing power, and inclusive friendships among all white
women is challenged. I was so depressed at how competitive everything felt—even with the kids."

> We are so socialized to compete with each
> other, we cannot even see each other.

For me, I learned that in order to uphold whiteness, I needed
to perform for my peers—appear nonthreatening, make them
laugh, and make friends and not enemies, so they would see me
as a good person. I was also the biggest girl in terms of size, so
appearing nonthreatening was a big deal for me. As long as I was
the quiet shy Black girl, I wouldn't stand out. I lived under the
false notion that I could have it all if I denied the parts of myself
that were seen as inferior or abnormal.

I worked hard for good grades but most teachers demonized
me for still not getting it right. Their demands for perfectionism,

which was not required of the white children in class, silenced me from seeing my true and highest self. Because on the white man's mythical stage, you will do anything to not be seen as inferior or othered. As I got older, I began to recognize my patterns of behaviors to seek approval by white folx. It wasn't until later in life, when I couldn't hold down a job and didn't really understand why, that I recognized the price one has to pay to stand on the white American stage is just not worth it. I had always been a disruptor, pointing out glitches in corporate settings. If the employee handbook wasn't in alignment with company practices, I'd either quit, call them out, or never go back. Oftentimes in those settings you're demonized for holding folx accountable. So rather than continue to perform, I chose a different path, one that ultimately led me to dismantle the stage I had been living on my whole life, the one that upholds whiteness.

THE STAGE OF WHITENESS

What I realized was that being on the stage of whiteness has driven me to deny my humanity and my human experience. The fact is, if life is a stage and I get to design it, I don't want nothing to do with this white cultural mythology sold to us by NBC, Bill Cosby, and the idea that if you work hard enough, the happy brownstone life will be yours, too. Because this mythology creates more harm than good; it makes individuals like myself have to work twice as hard to get nearly half of what our white counterparts are able to access and acquire.

According to Pew Research, "More than four-in-ten Americans say the country still has work to do to give black people equal rights with whites. A majority of adults say that being white helps people's ability to get ahead in the country at least a little (59%)...On the flip side, a majority (56%) sees being black as a disadvantage, with 25% saying it hurts people's ability to get ahead a lot."[1]

The myth of the American dream is the greatest lie in history. I am in no way attempting to discredit immigrants who have come to America and made this "dream" a reality. Many of my friends are sons and daughters of immigrants, and while they understand and appreciate their parents' sacrifice, vision, and efforts, they can also simultaneously acknowledge the white supremacy underlying the dream. In my lived experience as a Black woman in this country, the dream is harder to obtain than we think. For Black folx, it takes years of education, titles, and student loans for us to achieve a fraction of what others, including other marginalized communities, are able to attain. And as I found out, after a while, it just becomes exhausting trying to keep up with the Joneses. The performance of Black brilliance at the expense of self-sacrifice is simply not worth it.

In life, we all struggle with wanting to be seen and known, and when we perform for the white gaze, we end up in a competition among the marginalized-upon-marginalized in order to be recognized as special or different from others. We all have a desire to be chosen, to be loved, but when we tie our value to constructs of whiteness, we deny a piece of our humanity, choosing performance-based metrics of success over wholehearted healing and personal connection. This is why the work of antiracism cannot be fueled by performance but rather, it must be birthed through the full integration of our head, heart, and hands.

> You cannot move into co-conspiratorship
> until you dismantle your relationship with
> the white cultural stage.

Stepping off the stage of white culture means you must break up with the aspects and assumptions of whiteness that affect your behaviors. Judith H. Katz, a white thinker and organizational change analyst, developed a theoretical framework on the aspects and assumptions of white culture in the United States. It's well worth googling if you want to read about the entirety of her work, but for the sake of this discussion, what stuck out to me was the recognition of white culture's strict adherence to time, its rewarding of independence and autonomy, its prioritization of logic over emotions, its exercising of power *over* people versus power *with*, and its demonization of cultural practices or religions that are not "Christian."

Do any of those sound familiar? Do you find yourself struggling to see the connection? Friend, when you can begin to identify the ways you perform on the white cultural stage, you are then able to begin dismantling it. You can instead take the wood and build a path toward the collective liberation of all.

KEEPING UP WITH WHITE CULTURE

Breaking up this white cultural stage might sound easy but the reality is, it's not. As humans we desire to be loved, to be nurtured, to be noticed, and to be appreciated. But the interlocking systems of oppression have turned those authentic desires into a false narrative. Instead of desiring to be loved, nurtured, noticed, and appreciated, we crave being seen as better than, rooting all of our relationships in the supremacy Olympics. And in the white supremacy Olympics, everyone is fighting to be number one.

Instead of building deep and nuanced knowledge and community, we embrace the oversimplification of complex topics, risk our health and wellness to be noticed, and depend on likes and follows to fuel our self-esteem. The premise of the American dream teaches us we can have it all, whenever we want it, and on a silver platter. But if you're not in the top 10 percent of income-earners, we all have learned that is a big fat fib. And yet, despite Occupy Wall Street and Black Lives Matter, social media and its influence on culture has made the "American dream" popular again. Built on oppression, and impression management, social media is a performative space where people drag for likes, comments, and engagement in order to prove they have value—trying to get that famous blue check. In the marketing world, we call this impression management, which is the practice of subconscious and unconscious attempts to influence people by controlling information in their social interactions. Influencers build social equity by creating and enhancing their know, like, and trust factors.

There's a quote in marketing that goes, "All things being equal, people will do business with and refer business to those people they know, like, and trust."

Mark Schaefer, a social media marketing professor at Rutgers University writes, "People have something to say about the products and services they use, and they say it over online social networks to their friends and colleagues. As a result, business is again (1) personal and interactive, (2) quick and widely heard feedback, (3) reliance upon word of mouth recommendations, and (4) the ability to connect online with friends and new friends."

Don't get my words twisted. I am not suggesting that everyone on social media is fake and has nothing to offer. What I am saying is that folx who show up in the top 5 percent of the social media algorithm are usually white influencers who have curated their craft to increase their likability, earn your trust, and distract you from *your* work. And that same 5 percent tend to support Black lives in order to have a check cut, working to increase their social value in the global economy. This is why most of the amplification of melanated voices by white influencers failed, or they were called into by marginalized folx of color.

Most influencers utilize social media because they don't have to interact as themselves, wearing a persona that fuels their performance and their popularity. Social media has made it easy for us to fake it till we make it, to embody being a part of the culture and accepted by people across the world. As a co-conspirator, this level of influence is not necessary for the journey. You do not need to start a public blog, launch a paid book club, or teach a workshop after reading a book. You make a difference through your real-world action of laying down your power and sharing it with the marginalized majority. This work isn't about you being seen; it's about you unlearning, relearning, and allowing yourself to feel through the discomfort of the work. White culture will have you curating content for attention, rather than elevating the voices that actually matter.

I'm sure no one *wants* to keep up with white culture, but what I find is that if we don't keep up with white culture, we face being demonized and shamed for standing out and against these performance metrics of success. We tie our value to being seen and conforming to cultural norms that allow us to feel special. We perform out of the quest for perfection because perfection is a tenant of white supremacy culture, utilized as a qualifier of value. In Tema Okun's (another white thinker) white supremacy framework, she shares how perfectionism shows up in organizations. I've adapted the framework for an individual to see how their relationship with perfectionism can fuel performance in their everyday lives.

Folx who struggle with perfectionism strive to get credit for everything they do, so overperforming at work and at home is valued and appreciated.

Folx who are perfectionists also often see themselves as a problem, so when mistakes are made, they identify as the mistake, wearing a mask to perform for the likability of others, since they can't identify their own flaws without feeling they have failed the larger social pact. Because of this, perfectionists also have a hard time sitting in self-reflection, preferring to project themselves onto others.

DO NOW: Connect to Reflect. Phone a friend or someone who is on this healing journey with you. Ask them if they have a few moments for you to share what's coming up for you. Try asking them, "Do you have the emotional space to help me process my thoughts?" When given the green light, share some points of this book that are showing up for you and then ask your friend to reflect so you can connect to yourself.

The core root of the white allies' performance is tied to this need to be perfect. Their "work" can actually be seen as a performance of them holding themselves together, rather than an authentic unfolding to the journey. As long as we attempt perfectionism, we continue to perform on the stage of white culture. But performance is also a matter of ownership (and we know how white folx feel about owning shit), allowing the performer to control the narrative. Instead of allowing and unfolding, the work is to control and fix.

This notion of a mask reminds me of the first stanza in Paul Laurence Dunbar's poem "We Wear the Masks":

We wear the mask that grins and lies,
It hides our cheeks and shades our eyes,—
This debt we pay to human guile;
With torn and bleeding hearts we smile,
And mouth with myriad subtleties.

Why should the world be over-wise,
In counting all our tears and sighs?
Nay, let them only see us, while
We wear the mask.

We smile, but, O great Christ, our cries
To thee from tortured souls arise.
We sing, but oh the clay is vile
Beneath our feet, and long the mile;
But let the world dream otherwise,
We wear the mask!

This beautiful poem reminds us of how we wear a mask to disassociate from our true selves. What are the masks that you wear in your everyday life? I can tell you of three that I wear for sure: wife, mother, and public figure. The way I treat my husband is not the way I interact and treat my children. The way I interact with my children, I wouldn't dare interact with the public. These are three different distinct filters that I wear throughout my day. Psychotherapists and sociologists out there who uphold Westernized psychology, please note, I am using this as an example. No need to pathologize yourself or others on this journey.

So many of us hide behind the facade that everything is okay when it's not. We pretend to be on the same journey, but we struggle in isolation. We perform for others so we don't have to face ourselves. But when the work never proceeds past performance, it has no choice but to move right back to apathy. Because in order to be an action-driven co-conspirator, white allyship requires that you remove the mask and begin to deconstruct everything you thought you knew about identity, self, and yes, even, success.

PERFORMANCE CONSTRUCTS OF SUCCESS

Since the industrial revolution, we have believed that more is better, that folx should always be results-driven, and that all focus should be placed on rapid production for quicker turnaround to the end user. We've been trained overtime by social theories of performance to track goals and objectives, driven by corporate stakeholders who are determined to ensure a good return on investment. But the drive for results was never about having a better impact on humanity, but to have a better impact on the bottom line.

So on your healing journey, it would come as no surprise that you may have experienced a period of overconsumption of content to prove you're a good white person. For some of you, when marginalized stakeholders praised you for the bare minimum, you quickly ticked off the antiracism checkbox. Since you "crushed it," and the objective was met, you figured there was nothing more for you to learn or do. But adopting short-term performance metrics to a lifelong journey is rooted in capitalist white supremacy.

There are no quarterly earnings on justice.
There are no gold stars or performance-based
metrics for decolonization work.

This work is a lifelong journey and the action required is not rooted in how much you know but in what you do. Many of us are addicted to performance; we're hooked on the feeling we get from fitting in, being seen, and feeling known. In my workshop "Breaking the Addiction to Privilege," co-conspirators are blown away by seeing the concept of privilege as an addiction. According to the American Society of Addiction Medicine addiction is defined as "a treatable, chronic medical disease involving complex interactions among brain circuits, genetics, the environment, and an individual's life experiences. People with addiction use substances or engage in behaviors that become compulsive and often continue despite harmful consequences." According to researchers, addiction is a process that develops over time. But how can performance also be an addiction if it's merely an intellectual concept? Thing is, it's not. Performative behaviors can offer similar physical and emotional effects as getting high off a drug or a process disorder, like gambling or shopping. When we are enjoying the benefits of performance, we are experiencing a false positive, believing our joy or fulfillment is earned, but it is just as much of a mirage as any addictive substance or process.

Which is why when a white person is not living in Black skin, they are able to move into apathy as soon as the work gets uncomfortable. Because performance isn't a real investment of emotion or spirit; it is simply an empty reaction to feel better. Because you took a workshop, you assume that allows you to tap out and disengage whenever you want. It's like having a remote control; when the challenge gets boring, you can change it, turn it down, or turn it off. But you'll never know real power if you keep disconnecting from the source.

Many of us are addicted to the performance of presenting our faux self because since childhood, we've been socialized to be a good boy or girl. Part of that was being trained to be seen as an object or something of value and not as a whole human being. No wonder so many of us struggle to know ourselves because we spend more time performing our "selves" than being true to them. In the book *The Presentation of Self in Everyday Life,* Erving Goffman theorizes:

> When an individual comes in contact with other people, that individual will attempt to control or guide the impression that others might make of him by changing or fixing his or her setting, appearance, and manner. At the same time, the person the individual is interacting with is trying to form and obtain information about the individual.

Believing that all participants in social interactions are engaged in practices to avoid being embarrassed or embarrassing others, Goffman developed his dramaturgical analysis, wherein he observes a connection between the kinds of acts that people put on in their daily life and theatrical performances.

This theory suggests there is a connection between our daily life and the theatrical performances within it. It's actually connected to one of my favorite theories, self-presentation theory. If ya don't know, I am not a sociologist, but I love making connections between theoretical understandings of human life and our lived experiences of the work. According to this theory, "Self-presentation is an attempt to convey some information about oneself or some image of oneself to other people. It denotes a class of motivations in human behavior. These motivations are in part stable dispositions of individuals but they depend on situational factors to elicit them."

As sociologists Edward E. Jones and Thane S. Pittman once offered, individuals typically use five self-presentation tactics to communicate with others: self-promotion, ingratiation, supplication, intimidation, and exemplification. The question is, are we performing or are we moving through different emotions depending on the environments we're in? Understanding that you have a right to choose your path, friends, and social environments, I am drawn to conclude most of our relationships are performative. Because oppression has taught us that if an individual isn't a quiet contributor to the constructs of the white world, we get to choose when to cut them off.

You may have one Black friend but does that friend come from a different socioeconomic status than you? Also, though that same Black friend might be able to call you in about your racism, do they fear that calling you out on your colorblind beliefs or annoying "I love all people" rhetoric will sever the relationship? We struggle to get to know ourselves and each other outside of these social constructs of success. We live in a world where call-ins for accountability feel like an attack.

Accountability feels like an attack only when we aren't living into the work.

What's interesting is that it's easier to take accountability for intentional or obtuse harm or evidenced acts of racism, but what's really taboo is when we call in someone who is on the outside of "doing the work," while in truth, they are only upholding those interlocking systems of oppression through performative behaviors. It's so much easier to spot the devil when he's doing evil, but the real devil is the one offering the sweet fruit of allyship. For those of you who are choosing comfort over changed behavior, you aren't living out this journey.

But it's hard when we've been trained to handle our life as a movie. We can choose when to act, when to cut or end scenes, or edit the way we present ourselves in real time. Time and time again, allies choose when to act, when to end the journey, or edit the journey out of their lives. But this work isn't a movie, and it's certainly not a narrative written, directed, or starring whiteness. This is about Black life and death. If you're experiencing this work as though it is a movie, you may be compartmentalizing your journey as something separate from your real life. At some point, you must be ready to cut the show, and shift from performance and into authenticity. In fact, the next Black death requires it.

ACTION REQUIRES AUTHENTICITY

I don't want to introduce authenticity as a rigid practice but rather a fluid flowing experience. I define authenticity as being a genuine, real deal, honorable person. Authenticity begins when we can be true to ourselves without fear of judgment. It opens us to a level of self-intimacy, self-appreciation, and self-sustainability.

> Authenticity isn't a defined point;
> it is a learned practice requiring openness,
> isolation, grief, and growth.

As an antiracism guide, there was a moment when I moved away from my own authenticity. I found myself being on the hamster wheel of work and productivity. I signed up for all the interviews, went on all the podcasts, and raced to be number one, ghosting on workshops and valuing that blue check over the collective humanity of all. I perpetuated emotional exhortation to guilt white folx into the work rather than staying true to my own unique guidance of self/soul healing, knowing that the work requires nuanced relationship and restorative care.

I can call out performative behavior because there were moments during that Great Awakening and in the middle of the Shock and Awe, where I, too, performed. Not many people in the world will tell you their own business, but stories are liberatory. If you can see how I've moved through the work, it's my hope that you give yourself grace to get this work wrong, too. I came back to myself after my mother experienced a heart attack, and I went down to Mexico to spend some time away from the performance of self and back with myself.

It was through conversations with my partner and team that I began to recognize the ways I had been causing harm, and it was time to step into myself. It was time to move back into authenticity and out of performance-based leadership. But the moment I began to reclaim my authenticity, I began to lose worldly success and possessions. It was scary; losing shit always is. But I saw this as my ancestors calling me home to myself to connect on a soul level. By limiting distractions, I was able to recommit to the work. It felt as if things were falling apart, but sometimes we have to fall down to get back up. I could not hold space for others if I didn't do the hard and sometimes superficially unrewarding work of dropping into my authentic self.

Because here's the truth, I couldn't keep up with the perpetual performance; maybe some can, but I found it exhausting and at direct odds with the communal repair and soul care that is crucial to the work of guiding folx into healing.

When we tap into authenticity, we are able to embody spirit and hold space for others who are doing the same.

Authenticity allows us to keep and honor our commitments to the work we do personally and in the world. It requires us to be accountable to ourselves, to the collective, and to practice sustainable soul care. You know you're on the path of authenticity when your values reflect what you're living in your life. An authentic soul is moved into action through bravery and with clarity for the end goal of all.

MOVING INTO ACTION

It takes a brave soul to move into action, and action requires clarity. If you are not clear with your commitments, you will continually move away from doing the work of co-conspiratorship. Action in this work is fueled by authenticity, accountability, and self-sustainability. But in a world that shames authenticity and accountability, how can we be consistent in anything we do? That depends on you. If you are defining consistency based on society's terms, then you're in the constant cycle of upholding not-enough-ness.

The current system praises us for overworking and penalizes us for taking a break. It glorifies overcommitting and sacrificing our mental health for the sake of others. You must define consistency by what works for you, what feels good for your life. Many of you won't have the answer because you still don't know what life feels like outside the oppressive matrix. You haven't given yourself permission to drop into the feels of the work because you've been so consistent at performing, knowing the right things to say but not what to do.

But guess what? You get to choose how this journey will work for you, you get to have a say in what works for this season of your life, but because white folx have been told to suck up their feelings, you'll never take the risk to emote, which causes barriers to you taking real action for change. Instead you will say the right things, which only further cements the illusion of change on a machine that will not bend. But there are other barriers to growth. They include the fear of proximity, of doing this work wrong, of not knowing if you're an introvert, extrovert, or highly sensitive person, and of overconsuming information.

I can only assume you won't get proximate to the pain of those who hold marginalized identities because of time, bias, and whatever fears mainstream media has put into your head about communities of color. Many white folx avoid Black communities because movies such as *Boyz n the Hood* have instilled that all Black communities are inherently violent and unsafe. So the opportunity you may have to support Black-led movements in the hood are looked down upon because it's not a good fit for the work you do. As a white person in this work, good fits aren't an option. This isn't *The Hunger Games*. The odds will not work forever in your favor. You must know that this journey is less about your fears, and more about what you're willing to lay down to support the oppressed, the poor, the orphaned, the widowed, the unhoused, the single moms, the marginalized, the silenced, and the lost. When you recognize that fear is only false evidence appearing real, you can lean into the work a little more easily. Once you're clear on your intentions for entering this work, you'll recognize that ease is the way forward.

For some reason, action still seems to be the hardest part for the co-conspirator's journey. I am not sure what is the holdup; maybe you're expecting a manual on how to do it. The bad news is, this journey is individual and collective, so no manual is going to help you get it done. I believe many of you are so used to being told what to do, the idea of just doing, failing, or causing harm is scary and unnatural. But this work is soul work, and until you recognize that your soul requires you to grapple with the lessons of failure, you will repeat the same cycle of being stuck and unknowing.

What I have found is the more we know ourselves, the more we understand our relationship and challenges with taking action. Usually I would use a human designer to help us tap into our style of being, but since I'm not the expert, we can look at this from the introvert, extrovert, ambivert, and highly sensitive person (HSP) perspective. An introvert is someone who feels comfortable focusing on thoughts and ideas, rather than external action. Most folx who work behind the scenes of social movements are the introverts of the world.

Extroverts are sociable folx who tend to enjoy being out in the world. I call them the shake-and-bakers. They don't like to sit and think. They are the folx that protest on the front lines and show up for justice at the drop of the dime. An ambivert is someone who displays characteristics of both introvert and extroverts. These folx enjoy supporting on the front lines, the back end, and moving through all areas of the work.

And there are those who are highly sensitive persons. A highly sensitive person (HSP) is a term for those who are thought to have an increased or deeper central nervous system sensitivity to physical, emotional, or social stimuli. These individuals feel the weight of the world heavily and move better in nature, away from violence, and are promoting sustainable healing practices to regulate the journey of dismantling.

Understanding your personality style will help you find where you belong in the movement. As a co-conspirator, your responsibility is to act, but as my brother Jamal Taylor says, "Not in a performative way." Many co-conspirators seek quick fixes to large-scale problems. Until you audit your need to act, dismantle the stage that white supremacy has built for you, and understand your fit in the journey, you will stay on the hamster wheel of performative allyship.

But there is a way off.

Getting to the roots of performative activism will allow you to drop into yourself and truly heal. When you take the time and notice performance on your antiracism journey, you will begin to notice performance in other parts of your life. That is why this work is a healing journey, because you are able to find fractured pieces of yourself that are buried deep in the shadows. You have to get to the shadow to see the light, so visiting your relationship with performative activism will shine light on pieces of your journey you have never witnessed before.

REFLECTION QUESTIONS ON ACTION

· · · · · ·

1. What actions on your journey have been performative? How do you know? What is this information inviting you to learn or do?

2. Identify your personality type. How does this help you know where you fit in the movement?

3. Create a skills resume to give to BIPOC-led initiatives without expectations of building solidarity or solving any immediate problems. Your skills resume is a list of your talents that you can offer to BIPOC-led initiatives. After identifying your skills, write a letter and offer your time and experience to a nonprofit that can use your support.

· 7 ·

THE SWEET SPOT
OF SHAME AND
VULNERABILITY

"Shaming is one of the deepest tools of imperialist,
white supremacist, capitalist patriarchy because shame
produces trauma and trauma often produces paralysis."
—bell hooks

I bet you thought I'd open this chapter with a quote by Brené Brown, but as Maury Povich would say, the lie detector determined, *That was a lie!* In my culture, we use Maury as humor to bring in connection, curiosity, and the real to some very serious topics. Shout out to Brené Brown and her amazing work around shame and vulnerability (we'll hit that later in this chapter), but as a womanist, it is profoundly important to center Black educators, authors, and scholars' work around shame. This is how we normalize Black excellence and the liberatory experience.

I mean where do you think the notion of liberatory power comes from? Black People. *Period.* This quote by bell hooks was an accidental stumble-upon Google binge. You know how educators often go tell folx to Google the answer for yourself first. Well, I took my own advice. I was co-authoring community agreements for my learning community and Googled, "shame and Audre

Lorde," "shame and bell hooks," "shame and white supremacy," and I found this quote. It felt so surreal to read these words that stood at the heart of all of my teachings and understanding not only of white supremacy but of what stops us from engaging in the antiracist journey. In fact, this quote resonated so much for me, I've now used it twice in this book. White perfection would ask that I find a new quote, but soul work is about committing to the language of our liberation.

As co-conspirators, our goal is to move into collective action for that liberation, building new systems in a sustainable way, and centering the voices of Black, Brown, Indigenous, Southeast Asian, Asian American, Pacific Islander, and marginalized persons of color. This work is liberatory, as it moves us away from shame, and into the sweet spot of vulnerability. It roots us in self-expression and collective freedom where we work to activate our collective power. Liberatory power requires shame resilience, tapping into vulnerability and using the energy to expand rather than contract.

The goal of shame is to bring us into points of contraction, of power-loss, rather than expansion, of power-full.

Supremacy has taught all of us that shame is who we are, and that ideology has moved many folx into traumatic paralysis and a disjointed antiracist healing practice. This paralysis stops you dead in your tracks. What seemed like the opportunity for healing and growth turns into a spiral of shame because you "missed the mark" on action. Or you feel like a failure because you're constantly holding yourself and your healing journey up against white-supremacist standards of performance. This notion of failure leads to fragility, which eventually leads you to shame, and shame's job is to guilt you for not being good enough to persist toward your own healing. In order to be a true co-conspirator, you have to move with the shame, not away from it. The goal isn't to contract from the work; the goal is to integrate shame into the process of becoming vulnerable to the work.

It was December of 2018 when I booked my third in-person Check Your Privilege workshop in Marin, California. Marin County is one of the most racially segregated and wealthiest counties in Northern California, if not the country. I'm not gonna lie, I assumed that most folx came here to check the "good white person" box. So when I met Erika and Natalie, the event's organizers, through my good friend and co-conspirator Abby, I surprisingly had to put my own bias in check. You see, I, too, once struggled with the idea that white folx actually wanted to heal this stuff. Because in 2018, most white folx were living in the safety net of privilege. If they were called out, they didn't respond with grace and integrity, but defensiveness.

Books like *White Fragility* by Robin DiAngelo were the only tools in my toolbox I could give to white folx because they weren't trying to hear me. AT ALL. It's unfortunate that I believed the world worked this way, but white silence perpetuates white bias, and as I've shared, if it ain't white, it ain't right.

But to my surprise, Erika and Natalie really wanted to provide space for white folx in their community to begin the healing process. As spiritual teachers and healers, they knew that this work wasn't linear. So when workshop day came, I was surprised to see the energetic boundaries they set up for folx to stay curious and trust the process. I assumed the workshop would be held in some high-falutin' event space, so I had all my ducks in a row for this workshop. Name tags, workshop packets, and notes to keep me on topic. When I arrived at the space, however, I was surprised to see a beautiful home in the redwoods of Marin. The energy was earthy and moving. I remember seeing the beauty of the trees, and at that moment, I knew the energy of the space would move us from organized planned-out content into a space for authentic community connection and dialogue.

During the workshop, we practiced a specific exercise to peer process their relationship with privilege. I can't even count how many times folx have *shoulda, woulda, coulda* themselves to death when they feel like they have failed to heal their relationship with racism. In that moment, the shame spiral can become activated but that day in the room, my response was, "When you find yourself overthinking, shaming yourself, becoming overcritical, you must remind yourself to fuck the patriarchy. Everyone, say it out loud: 'Fuck the patriarchy.'"

Everyone shouted in response, "Fuck the patriarchy!" In that moment, I could see that when you own up to shame, and move with it, you can drop into the work. This isn't to say that you will always have movements of breakthroughs, but rather that when you sit with the discomfort and spiral outward, rather than inward, you can affirm yourself in a way that moves from paralysis and into the embodiment of the work.

SHAME AS A TOOL OF SUPREMACY

As Audre Lorde once wrote:

> For the master's tools will never dismantle the master's house. They may allow us temporarily to beat him at his own game, but they will never enable us to bring about genuine

change. And this fact is only threatening to those women who still define the master's house as their only source of support.

Can I get an Amen? Shout out to the ancestors for this mighty word. Friend, if you're in this work and you think shaming yourself into existence is gonna work, sorry to tell you, but you're doing this work hella wrong. Shame can be defined as a feeling of embarrassment or humiliation that arises in relation to the perception of having done something dishonorable, immoral, or improper. And it is one of many tools, and one of the most powerful, in the white supremacy toolbox. This toolbox is full of contrivances developed to uphold white American values, goals, and objectives. I have stated them before but I will share them again: the constructs of rugged individualism, all-or-nothing thinking, competition between women (especially Black women), the demonization of marginalized cultures, and the glorification of Western Christianity.

We uphold these tools in our everyday lives through unconscious and repetitive behavior. But each of these behaviors must be interrogated one thought at a time, so we can remove these old manipulations and create a new toolbox. Supremacy requires we deny our feelings and emotions. It trains us to disassociate with anything that is outside of the intellect; we replace feelings and emotions with high-value quantitative analysis. And anyone who does feel is seen as a loser in a system where the highest score always wins. But when we deny our own humanity, we lose pieces of ourselves along the way, spiraling us into shame.

We must not forget that shame leads to repression, repression leads to depression, and depression leads to our anxiety.

And anxiety keeps us in a hyper-aroused state, living in fight, flight, or freeze. We are constantly bombarded with messages about being our best self, feeling all the good feelings, having high vibrations, and more. What we fail to realize is that this work is about becoming, healing, and unsettling. It is the shadow work and the frequency work that is necessary for us to be able to drop into ourselves.

As Helen Lewis writes, "The feeling of shame can be described as a sense of smallness, worthlessness, and powerlessness in any given situation. It is triggered by a 'perceived' break in one's con- nectedness to others or to oneself." When we feel disconnected to ourselves, we cannot attune or attach ourselves to those around us. If you're in a shame spiral, it's hard to connect because you are disassociated from yourself, looking instead for the right supremacy fix to feel better. Shame is not just a thought process, it is an embodied experience, and like trauma, it's an energy that can become stuck in our bodies for life.

To move with shame, we need to address it as a somatic expe- rience that affects our ability to connect our heads, hearts, hands, and bodies. For example, when you experience shame associated with the fear of "getting something wrong," you may find yourself calling yourself a name, and then ending it with "I should have known better." When we experience the feelings of shame, we often gaslight ourselves, eventually reverting back to "good vibra- tions" to suppress any negative thoughts, or our capacity to au- thentically feel.

The interlocking systems of oppression have trained us to have a disconnected relationship with feelings and emotions, so though many have experienced shame, they have learned to sup- press it as part of life's performance. But when your thoughts or feelings are disconnected, you will likely begin to feel a heaviness in your body; it is the knowing that this isn't a new experience. As we discussed, our former stories and traumatic experiences have memories in our DNA. When we sit with shame in our bodies, we are not only echoing the past, we are threatening the future with this cultural cycle of repression and depression.

On your healing journey, repression and shame in relation to racism can feel hopeless. Because there are no easy answers, it is easy to allow the shame to become suffocating, heavy, painful, and overwhelming. If you already don't know how to work with shame, you will be constantly pulled away from this work.

DO NOW: Paint and create. When we tap into our imagination, we are able to connect to play. Get out of your head and into your heart by grabbing some finger paints and butcher paper and paint to the "Heal Your Way Forward" playlist on Spotify. After the painting dries, take a look and ask yourself what are the common themes that come alive in your painting?

When you get into the cycle of repression, old memories of the past can rob you of any joy. Since shame is known as an avoidance response, its job is to make all of us feel worthless and immobile. As a white person, you are not innately taught how to move with shame. But in my humble opinion, we only duplicate oppression by naming your feelings of guilt as "white shame." By tying the social constructs of race to your experience, supposedly, it helps you identify your shame and guilt as tied to your whiteness. But before I start sounding like the "All Lives Matter" crowd, let me just say this. You wouldn't name my shame, or my experience, Black shame or Black guilt, so why would you connect your shame and guilt on this journey to an extended label? That keeps the focus of this journey on you, and ascribes you to a binary of good or bad. That's the problem with the interlocking systems of oppression: We can't even see how we oppress each other with the language we use to heal.

You have been socialized to believe that shame means you are a bad person, that you are your shame. Shame is your "not good enough" voice, working to reinforce supremacy by evaluating your behavior. You've learned to gaslight yourself from the system causing you to contract from the world by hyperfocusing on fixing yourself, as if *you* are a problem. You are not broken or something to be fixed. You are learning and relearning, and that is growth on the edge of life. Shame wants you to contract, keeping you from seeing who you really are. Its dark presence makes being in this work so uncomfortable that you'd rather lean into the benefits of privilege. You must began to encourage yourself to move with the shame and not against it.

> Moving against shame is complicity in the
> white supremacist world in which we live.

But to move with it, you have to recognize that you are not your shame. Vulnerability is where the sweet spot begins and shame doesn't necessarily end, but is easier to work through. When you finally decide to tap into vulnerability, you are on the path toward your healing. It is then that you will finally recognize shame as a tool of distraction, not as something you are. Vulnerably moving with shame is the only way you can walk forward on this journey.

EMOTIONAL VULNERABILITY IS THE SWEET SPOT

I struggle with being vulnerable. I mean, hell, we all do. As early as seven years old, media and life experiences reinforced the message that I had to be a strong and hard Black girl and, essentially, a strong Black woman even though I was still a child.

I was too sucked up to deal with life. Instead, I believed that in order to become someone of importance I had to center the white American dream as my reality. As a youth, I became a spokesperson for the girls in my middle school, not because it was cool or popular, but because "U.N.I.T.Y." by Queen Latifah was my girl-power fight song and I wanted to stand up against the boys who were mean to girls. Even in my music choices, I was empowered to fight as a Black youth, though it was at the risk of normalizing Black woman anger and hardness. But the one thing I was not allowed was to feel into myself.

Softness is something that is taught, and throughout history, Black women have never had the time nor space to experience joy, pleasure, gentleness, or to tap fully into their divine feminine energy.

The Bible, which is the oldest and most successful tool of Western oppression, taught me that anything that represents an embodiment of my ancestral practices was evil. Thanks to the interlocking systems of oppression and Westernized Christianity, I would have been seen as a "Jezebel" for wanting to embody the fullness of myself. Jezebel was a queen in the Old Testament who caused hella harm to the children of Israel. Essentially she was a "sinner" and her name is evoked throughout Christianity as someone who is dominating and controlling and engages in immorality, idolatry, false teaching, and unrepentant sin. There are some characteristics of Jezebel that ain't cool, but if she was evil 'cause she had power and autonomy over herself, then that's a whole damn misogynist issue on its own.

Until early adulthood, I was trained to not ask questions, do what I was told, and suck up my tears. Knowing what I know now, in order to protect my psychological and emotional safety in this white man's world, I could not experience the full anatomy of a soft, more embodied womanhood. Going back to my ancestors in enslavement, they were humiliated, exploited, oppressed, overworked, and undervalued. Any sign of emotion could come at the cost of losing one's life. As a Black woman, in an imperialist, white supremacist, patriarchal world, vulnerability was a threat, which is why we were not only not taught it, but also forced to unlearn it.

But today, that process is being reversed. I have seen that you can learn vulnerability. Through rest, through allowing love to flow through me and my life, through how I treat and love myself, I am learning and relearning how to stand in the power of my own softness, giving myself grace for being human.

I am vulnerable when I am not on the cycle of comparing myself or my path to others. I am vulnerable when I can hold myself with compassion and root myself to love. I am vulnerable when I can admit that I am still learning and unfolding and failing and feeling.

And it is well worth it.

EMOTIONAL VULNERABILITY

In the co-conspirator's healing toolbox, emotional vulnerability is the tool that replaces the master's constructs. It encompasses love, liberation, freedom, autonomy, empathy, self-compassion, and the practice of becoming. As you become a co-conspirator, you recognize that the master's tools no longer work for you, so you let go of isolation, perfectionism, and apathy and move into love, self-compassion, and empathy. It might sound like a dream, but I can tell you from experience, it's absolutely possible.

So what is emotional vulnerability? To me, it's the practice of allowing yourself to expose your deepest insecurities, feelings, and thoughts. You say how you feel and what you need and name the desires of your heart. It's not "emotional vomiting"—throwing your junk on somebody to guilt them or manipulate them; rather, emotional vulnerability is the practice of being yourself. In the oppressive world in which we live, we don't know how to just be ourselves. We are trained to be what the world wants us to be, and to think like the majority, because fear of the minority is stepping out of normalcy and into difference.

A majority of us live our lives on the path of least resistance, not willing to risk our identity to be who we are called to be. Because to become that person requires we risk emotional vulnerability, rejecting the social constructs that tell us who we are supposed to be.

The benefit of vulnerability is that when we put it into practice, we allow a softness to open us up to the world. My homegirl (well, not for real, but one day), Dr. Brené Brown, describes emotional vulnerability as "the birthplace of love, belonging, joy, courage, empathy, and creativity." Unlike shame, vulnerability is the expansion of this work, not its contraction. When you love yourself or are focused on loving yourself, you allow yourself to access that softness, or as my therapist Jeff says, "Dropping into love and vulnerability is the sweet spot."

Usually when we are "fighting against" the interlocking systems of oppression, we are not thinking about love and vulnerability. But we end up moving with the system when we choose to fight against it. Because the system makes no room for self-compassion, mistakes, courage, or empathy. The system demonizes anyone or anything working against it.

> The goal isn't to fight the system, the goal is to liberate yourself from it, by not duplicating its constructs in your own work.

When we deny our humanity or fail to have self-compassion or self-empathy, we are merely upholding oppression. We are trained to give ourselves to others, but when was the last time you gave yourself to you?

It's easy to contract, but when it comes to giving yourself grace to expand into vulnerability, it can be difficult. Who taught you that you had to give so much? Where did you learn not to cry? How did you begin to devalue yourself? These are the questions that can help you recall the moments that being vulnerable was a sin and you were to do as the systems tell you. It is very isolating to want to feel your way through, only to be told to suck it up and keep going. The need for your emotional vulnerability is a critical tool in the work toward freedom.

LIBERATORY LOVE

As a co-conspirator, you cannot move forward in this work without the practice of emotional vulnerability and empathy. Empathy is a practice that allows you to see and share the feelings of another. It allows you to not be isolated in this work, to see and notice you are not alone and that others are willing to share a piece of their journey with you. Empathy gives you courage to continue this healing work, because there's liberation when you see yourself in someone else's story. The vulnerable and empathic connection you make with others will move you from the supremacy of isolation into liberatory love.

You cannot do this work unless it's rooted in allowing yourself to be seen and known, until you are able to drop into love's liberation. And you cannot do this work in isolation. You might have been trained to do everything on your own, to be number one, to not depend on anyone for anything, but this belief doesn't make space for vulnerability. And it doesn't make space for healing. Isolation is the brewing space for perfectionism, shame, and guilt. How can you be vulnerable alone? How can you see yourself in your own story, if you are always fighting to be perfect and have it all together? Make that make sense, as my friend Louiza "Weeze" Doran would say. Because the math ain't mathin'.

Isolation does not make space for vulnerability; isolation is where shame and guilt impacts your ability to move, feel, give love, and be cared for. There's no space for vulnerability in isolation. Vulnerability requires self-attunement. You have to have the skills to restore your sense of self, but first, you need to put them into practice and practice that work in community.

In our Check Your Privilege community, we have learned to teach and learn the practices of vulnerability, connection, and compassion. We have no systemic approach to this work. Rather, we move with the shame and place vulnerability at the center of our journey. We allow shame to be our teacher, and action to be the driving catalyst of the work we do in the world. In our community, we teach grace, empathy, and how to honor the waves of shame in this process. In fact, we allow shame to be a force of action, versus paralysis, and in doing so, we deny white supremacy its most powerful tool, reshaping it into one used for healing instead of harm.

We practice awareness of what we feel in every moment, by disengaging from the intellect and tapping into the somatic experience, the integration of the heart and hands in this work. Emotional vulnerability is a necessary spiritual practice in our community, as it allows all of us to be present to the lessons we need to keep moving forward. It is a space to process, practice, and push through our ways of knowing to co-create a better community.

Your individual work is to allow shame to be your teacher, to drop into self-compassion and vulnerability. When we move with shame, we don't have time to wallow in what was, to stay trapped in white supremacy's history. Here is our chance to heal forward.

REFLECTION QUESTIONS ON SHAME AND VULNERABILITY

· · · · · ·

1. In what ways have I allowed shame to stop me from seeing my own magic?

2. Why is it so hard for me to be vulnerable on my journey toward healing?

3. How can I be attuned to myself to know when I am leaning out of vulnerability?

DID YOU GHOST?
GOOD, NOW RECOMMIT

"Failure actually helps you to recognize the areas
where you need to evolve. So fail early,
fail often, fail forward."
—Will Smith

There have been days when I have thought about throwing my own work away. Nothing fuels my desire to ghost more than seeing other folx disappear from their own healing journeys. We all know what it means to be ghosted by a friend or a lover, when someone suddenly disappears with no explanation. But I got to tell you, it cuts the same way when you watch white people replicate the same process in their antiracism work. Because what they're basically saying is, *I don't want to help save your life anymore, but I don't have the guts to tell you that straight to your face.*

What's even worse is when the ghosting happens on a mass scale, or what I call the Great Unsubscribe. This is when white folx temporarily engage in the work, then unsubscribe, ghost, or leave as if there is nothing left to learn. Not gonna lie, but I've dreamed of doing the same thing, packing up the fam, moving to Mexico, and not looking back. In those moments, I have to remind myself that this work is ultimately for me, for my life, for my healing, and it's not about the number of subscribers or co-conspirators I engage. Because beyond me, it's for those who remain or recommit even if they've ghosted the process. And when that happens, I am reminded that this work is a called and chosen work. I recall who is committed and who has helped me in my way forward. And I remember that leaving and returning to the work is often part of the process, including my own.

Leaving is a privilege that I am worthy to have. Modeling re-commitment isn't easy when you've struggled with attachment and intimacy issues, but it can be learned and practiced over time. For me, whenever I feel pulled to give up the work, I consider the complexities of a spiritual journey. I remember my days partici-pating in the choir at New Hope Missionary Baptist Church, in Dekalb, Illinois. That church in the middle of cornfields provided an awakening in my life when I needed it most. I will never forget Thursday night choir rehearsals, which were a lifeline to push through difficult times. Reverend Pringle would sing the gospel song "Stand," belting out in his deep baritone voice the reminder that no matter what happens, when we feel like we can't do any-thing more, all we can do is stand.

Goosebumps would and still cover my body as I remember the energetic resonance of those words. They would move me to tears as a higher energy called me to trust the process, to stay committed and lean on the promise that through belief in a higher source, which at that point in my life was God, everything would work itself out. That song was the hope for a better future, reminding me to stand tall and know that although the world feels and looks bleak, we can always connect into a deeper en-ergy, no matter the external forces or influences of the world out-side those church doors.

But just as with my antiracism journey, I struggled to stay connected to church, ghosting it and anything connected to it, time and time again. Then again, for me church was also tied to pain, shame, and guilt. I couldn't ignore Western Christianity's connection to hypocrisy, gossip, and slander, and the broken trust and ruined friendships I had experienced within the church only further fueled my discomfort. It was just easier to walk away from the pain then move through the journey. Instead of seeing discomfort as the teacher, I allowed it to push me away from my spirituality. But that's the challenge of discomfort. When you don't have the tools to stay committed to the process, or when you're turned off by something in the process, it's a lot easier to ghost.

WE ALL GHOST

When working with co-conspirators, there is the one truth I have to hold close: We all ghost. But when it happens to you, it's hard to have empathy for the process. Much like the process of ghosting, it's just easier to present ourselves as a wounded soul than to navigate and move with the shame of being ghosted. We put the shame on the person who disappeared rather than feel the hurt and disappointment that comes when it happens to us.

So think about it, when was the last time you were ghosted? For me, it depends on the context. In terms of an intimate relationship, I'd say eight years ago or so. In terms of folx I've had the pleasure to work with on this journey . . . it happens every day.

Does it hurt? Absolutely.

Can I do anything about folx choosing to walk away? Nope.

It takes wisdom to know when to not let
others' actions influence how you see yourself
and the work you are called to do.

But when you realize being ghosted is never really about you, it doesn't sting as much. On one's journey you may see ghosting as a way to disconnect with the reality of upholding interlocking systems of oppression. In my book *Check Your Privilege*, longtime co-conspirator Britney describes her ghosting as focusing on everything else but the work ahead. She says, "Ghosting is the act of abruptly halting communication with someone. Or in my case, no longer actively participating in my antiracism work. I stepped back and focused on everything else, anything else. As I waited for my bruised ego to heal, I shirked away from anything that had to do with racism and antiracism. Because without racism, there is no antiracism, and when reading about one always led to the other, both ended up pointing to me as a complicit party that perpetuated racism and white supremacy."

Britney lost interest in the work because she was unable to move with the shame, preferring to avoid the facts of her own complicity rather than moving toward the hard work of healing. On her journey she noticed that everything in her life had suddenly become about racism and she did not want to face the reality that this was the world we live in. Rather than face herself, she avoided commitment and connection and chose to extract herself from the process. As a white person, it's easy to opt out or walk away especially if you aren't committed and connected to it in a deeply intimate way. The more you are invested, the less shame has power over your process.

For so many members of the co-conspirator collective, ghosting has been used readily as a tool to escape shame. In fact, the shame spiral would become so uncomfortable, many folx chose to hyper-focus on other areas of their life in order to avoid their healing journey. For some, they hyper-focused on their careers while others focused on their children. A couple of individuals opted out altogether, not grasping the concepts and how to apply them to their lives.

While some ghost out of feeling too much, there are others who ghost because they feel apathetic. With so much trauma porn, they've been desensitized to the call to action. They run out of energy to respond to injustice, becoming so apathetic that whatever initially drew them in (a police shooting, micro- or macro-aggressions at work, a challenging relationship with a friend) will ultimately also drive them to leave.

For some, they go too hard too fast. They find themselves in the hyperarousal of anxiety, caused by unconsciously consuming and intellectualizing so much information, that they tire themselves out from continuing forward on the journey. This phenomenon is known as learners' fatigue, as co-conspirators are rapidly trying to learn new skills to be a better version of themselves. Rather than taking the journey in bite-size pieces, they rush the process, leading to burnout, stress, and eventually self-sabotage.

DO NOW: Meditate. As we intellectualize this process, we may run against shame and discomfort on the journey. Take five minutes and meditate on your journey. Close your eyes, turn on a meditative audio guide if you have one, light a candle, and be still with this practice, with all the things you are learning and unlearning.

I believe as humans, we are never satisfied. We have been socialized to not attach securely to anything that challenges our comfort, which is why we struggle to stay committed to a process—any process. We have multitasked ourselves into trying to hyper-focus on work, life, family responsibilities, pleasure, exercise, meditation, belief systems, friendships, social media, errands, hobbies, life pursuits, and we lose our ability to commit fully to anything. When you add technology to that mix, you've created a recipe for failure. It may be true that our minds have unlimited potential, but living in an imperialist, capitalist, white suprema-cist world, there is no time or space to detach or to commit to the process for the long haul. Supremacy says move quickly onto the next thing, keep up with the Joneses, and you'll have all you need. We're so busy attaching to anything for the sake of saying we are a part of something, that we aren't able to attach in a way that deep commitment requires and that change demands.

If ever you have wondered why our country has yet to experi-ence a full-scale revolution, this is why. We might join the march for a day or two, we might send some letters or make some calls, but it's hard to put your life, comfort, welfare, and resources on the line for something when you can barely make time to commit past next month.

Commitment requires consistency, and we can't give what we don't have. That's why I've learned to not expect white folx to be committed to this process if they aren't thoughtfully engaged in why they are doing it. They may be interested in it, but interest doesn't equate to commitment. Commitment requires intimacy, and for many people, intimacy is hard. But if you aren't experi-encing intimacy in your relationships, how can you experience intimacy in this work? Most folx don't recognize how their rela-tionships with commitment and intimacy get mirrored in anti-racism work, because if we don't love ourselves enough to be intimate and committed to others, how can we love ourselves enough to be willing to do this work? That's why so many people ghost as soon as they get disinterested, because interest simply isn't enough to hold them when the hard stuff starts to show up, and the hard stuff will always show up.

COMMITMENT VS. INTEREST

Interest is defined as the state of wanting to learn about something or someone. Commitment is being dedicated to that process. You may have come into this work because the death of Breonna Taylor sparked your "interest" in injustice, but you weren't necessarily committed. You were curious about what the work was but you were not necessarily ready to make that interest a lifelong process. In order to heal forward, you must commit fully, or re-engage when you recognize that you viewed this work as an interest, and not as a commitment.

Author and motivational speaker Dr. Ken Blanchard offers this powerful thought on the topic: "There is a difference between interest and commitment. When you're interested in something, you do it only when it's convenient. When you're committed to something, you accept no excuses, only results."

You're not committed if you drop out when things get hard. In order for you to stay in this work, you must assess what you are willing to risk to stay a part of the process. This work is inviting you to lay down your power, risk relationships, learn new thought processes, and give up comfort in order to be in a constant state of presence. You are being invited to a new level of emotional intimacy and a connection to a work greater than you will ever know.

White folx fear intimacy because you have
been trained to disconnect from anything that
might build real and powerful community.

Patriarchy works best when we isolate ourselves from each other. Patriarchy shames connection and rewards rugged individualism. So when we experience a connection that feels real and raw, especially one motivated by violence, we attune to each other's needs. This is why in 2020, during the early days of COVID, the hyperawareness and circulation of Black death awakened us and connected us across racial differences. This is why we protested together, why we called out our employers, why we demanded justice. And yet once that initial pop occurred, white folx's sense of shame kept them from committing to the process.

In the months and year that followed, I kept wondering, how did we get there? How do we always move from this deep sense of commitment and connection right back to the place of disconnection from which we started? As I said, as soon as any sense of "American normalcy" returned—you know, getting rid of the evil president, the excitement around the COVID-19 vaccine authorizations, the rushing to get our kids back in school full-time—we began to disconnect from the attunement to the work. Almost overnight, we lost interest in our commitments. Black guides like myself watched huge chunks of our followers and subscription members fade away within months. People who had been posting and commenting and engaging were suddenly gone. Instead, we watched as their profiles swiftly reverted back to business, productivity, and other social contracts of success. Which led me to question, were they ever really committed or were they just interested?

It is an American, or rather "white cultural," instinct to move with urgency when we are working toward upholding systemic oppression. Considering the pandemic was the awakening needed to reset the industrial world and ourselves, the government panicked when it could no longer function as it needed to. The powers that be never intended for us to rest. Since the beginning of the industrial age (and arguably the centuries leading up to it), their hamster wheel of oppression has kept us fighting to find security. In terms of the American dream, security has been defined by the big house, nice cars, and overworking ourselves into over-exhaustion. And in the process, what other option do we have but to become disconnected from humanity? The government knows that too many of us awakening to our own power would cause an overthrow of their imperialist system.

This is the dance of patriarchy. Some moments it creates a false sense of connection, and other times, it plays a game of dominance. In *The Will to Change*, bell hooks writes, "Psychological patriarchy is a 'dance of contempt,' a perverse form of connection that replaces true intimacy with complex, covert layers of dominance and submission, collusion and manipulation."[1] This reminds us that the dance of patriarchy stops us from feeling an intimate connection to a cause, maintaining dominance through our collusion with the system and manipulation versus arriving into true connectedness. I believe that in order to reintegrate this work, we need to connect the dots on how commitment, intimacy, and passion can fuel our dedication to the movement and to the dismantling of the patriarchy, which consistently interrupts that dedication with its own emergency programming.

COMMITMENT, INTIMACY, AND PASSION

White supremacy will never support intimacy, which is what ultimately blocks folx from being embodied in this work. Since supremacy thrives on lack of commitment, intimacy, and passion, it shouldn't surprise you when people ghost the work. They don't ghost because it's taboo, but rather because the systems of interlocking oppression will begin to do their own ghost whispering, offering them messages that they are being manipulated, unseen, not heard, or devalued. Some people ghost because they have been told that they have no space to be in the movement, so there's no need for connection.

For some, they've been so hyper-focused on using their power to call folx into the work rather than building connections with people in the work that they become easy targets for supremacist messaging, which tells them that they are failing at this work, and there is nothing worse than failing in white supremacist culture.

But a movement fueled by commitment, intimacy, and passion is critical to staying committed to the healing journey of a co-conspiratorship. Ultimately, intimacy is the language that allows us to understand vulnerability, openness, and sharing. To be in this work, you must be able to connect with others on an empathic level, moving away from the supremacist agenda and toward collective consciousness.

But for so many of us, we don't even understand what intimacy means. The reality is I was today-years old when I learned that there are six types of intimacy that individuals need to feel committed and connected to a person, place, or thing. I won't touch on all of them here, but I do want to discuss four forms that can help you determine the level of intimacy you need for your journey:

- Physical intimacy, which includes touch, is established to feel a healthy connection between two people.
- Emotional intimacy is offered through our words or communication. Though this type of intimacy requires a level of empathy in order to establish a connection, it produces a deep resonance between people.
- Creative intimacy is the practice of self-expression through art projects and physical and self-expressive modes of connection, allowing us to express ourselves with greater passion. I think for many people, this can be why they get disengaged from their antiracism work. Because we so often think of learning as an intellectual process, we fail to create a more embodied experience. After the Great Awakening, so many people were using their screens to engage, they weren't able to collaborate through creative intimacy in order to make the work more actioned and embodied. The many workshops, as well-intentioned and thoughtful as they might have been, likely felt like another job, just another thing to learn versus an opportunity to connect and move through.
- Experiential intimacy occurs when two people are engaged in the same activity at the same time, physically creating something together. It would almost seem like 2021 was an invitation to experimental intimacy, except for there have been so many false starts at physical connection that much of that work has been delayed. Not surprisingly, as these opportunities for intimacy have been interrupted by COVID spikes and social distancing, the initial interest in the work has waned.

Friends, I can't say that I have the answers here but I do know that when there is commitment, intimacy, and passion, people don't ghost this process. Because as much as I have seen people disappear from this work, I have also watched many others stay. If you are to continue your journey forward, you must find your ways into these concepts in order to commit and recommit to the process.

Without passion, you will not be able to pursue justice. Without passion, you will not be able to stay in this work. And without passion, you will not be able to embody an experience of intimacy and connection that allows you to drop into the vulnerability required on your journey forward. There's a good chance you don't even know that you have an aversion to commitment or intimacy or passion. It could have been that you have a childhood trauma that has not allowed you to create proper attachments, which has made it easier to let go of the work because you aren't even sure how to establish authentic connection.

I've come to learn that if you are going to really embody something, you have to know the ways in which you are attuned and attached to it. Without knowing your attachment style, how can you know the ways in which the pursuit of commitment, intimacy, and passion could work for you as a co-conspirator on your healing journey.

I am here to remind you that part of doing the work is getting it wrong. If you feel like you've failed or that you've moved off the path of your journey, or that you haven't gotten the work right, I am going to invite you to come back to yourself, but also, to come back to the process. Recall where you went wrong and recommit to the work.

Is recommitting easy? Hell no. Have you ever had to call someone up who you ghosted? You not only have to apologize, you have to explain why you disappeared and you have to figure out how to make it right moving forward. This is and can be incredibly humbling work, but that doesn't mean it's humiliating. Quite the opposite.

> In recommitting, you are showing that you can be a person of integrity, you can source your passion and intimacy, and you can pick yourself up and continue to fail forward, even when this journey feels impossible or difficult, especially when it does.

Yes, you can pick up you privilege pass and tap out when you want, but just remember that pass is what makes you not only complacent but also complicit. It takes next-level motivation to re-engage in this work, but often those that can find the intimacy and passion to recommit are the greatest catalysts for healing and liberation.

RECOMMITMENT

In conversations with co-conspirators, recommitment is often discussed as the hardest part of the journey. The shame spiral can take you on a mind-bending journey of self-awareness, which is why the fear of getting the work wrong can make you want to ghost when it feels like too much. But people struggle with recommitment because they're afraid to admit when they were wrong or to make amends for any harm caused. Many of you stay on the wheel of the good/bad binary, with that voice in your head saying, "Since I will be seen as a bad white person, I won't admit my harm. I will just come back as if nothing ever happened."

It's the inconsistency that's a challenge for me, because inconsistency won't allow you to recommit to anything. I'm not a doctor (yet) nor do I play one in real life, but I do know that the theory of attachment styles come from a social-psychological framework. It's rooted in the belief that our adulthood connections are shaped by our childhood experiences. This theory suggests that each of us dwells in one or more multiple domains of attachment. According to the Richmond Psychotherapy Attachment and Trauma Institute:

> There are three primary, underlying dimensions that characterize attachment styles and patterns. The first dimension is closeness, meaning the extent to which people feel comfortable being emotionally close and intimate with others. The second is dependence/avoidance, or the extent to which people feel comfortable depending on others and having partners depend on them. The third is anxiety, or the extent to which people worry their partners will abandon and reject them.

I don't find it coincidental that our early childhood experiences are connected to our commitments as adults. It goes back to socialization—we are who we are based on our lived experiences. One can never truly understand how or why they are in this work, if they haven't looked back and interrogated their patterns of consistency, commitment, intimacy, and attachment over their lifetime. I cannot tell you how to determine your attachment style, so before you go into a Google binge, I recommend that you request support from a clinical social worker. But before you sit down in a therapist's chair, you must first be open to un-learning and relearning yourself.

For some, you may have childhood wounds you are not willing to see, or maybe you could be reading this and struggling with how to connect it to the past. Newsflash: True healing occurs when you can view your past as a teacher and challenge yourself to embrace the healing it offers. Just because your family socialized you to be a certain way, whether they offered secure or insecure attachments as part of their love, you don't have to stay that way. Even if commitment or intimacy is scary to you, the fear doesn't need to stunt your growth.

You cannot be passionate on this journey if you can't access the spaces in your life where you refuse to drop in. This is not a message of love and light; this is an invitation to drop into your shadow and see what is on the other side, waiting for you to begin to heal. Many of you don't want to get below the surface of your work because you are scared. You are living out stories that were formed in systems of oppression, perpetuated in your youth and through adulthood to keep you on the cycle of hyperactivity. The idea is that if you just do enough, put your kids in enough activities, keep yourself so busy you can barely breathe, you will be able to stay afloat. But what drowning person survives by flailing their arms and failing to breathe? When you are truly ready to heal, to surrender to your past, you commit to giving up those old stories and building a new pathway along your journey.

Healing is your birthright, and for every opportunity you take on this journey to heal a piece of yourself, you heal seven generations forward and backward. The invitation into co-conspiratorship is one of acceptance, commitment, community, and engagement. Remember, even when you ghost the process, there's space to come back and begin again.

Your job isn't to self-sabotage when you ghost, it's to recommit. Like Dorothy In *The Wizard of Oz*, you get to return home and wake up after falling asleep in the opium fields of white supremacy. You will endure struggles on your path to recommitment, but eventually you will become awake enough to continue forward even when obstacles emerge. And over time, you will meet folx who want to walk with you, others who are striving imperfectly to be in liberation for themselves and others. This recommitted path will teach you that this work requires relationships. But if you are going to commit to it, the relationships along the way must be sustainable, accountable, and nourishing to your path forward. As a co-conspirator, you have full autonomy to heal, change, and grow. In order for you to truly be in this work, you have to know that ghosting isn't a sign of failure but rather an invitation to look at yourself in a more meaningful way.

That is how we commit to healing, intimately and passionately, every day.

REFLECTION QUESTIONS ON RECOMMITMENT

• • • • • •

1. What does commitment look like to me on my antiracism journey?

2. If commitment feels scary to me, what do I need to look at in order to heal my fear of commitment?

3. Where did I first learn to escape or avoid intimacy? Am I willing to do the work and rebuild my intimacy muscle?

· 9 ·

THE WORK REQUIRES RELATIONSHIPS

"The larger your beloved community, the more you
can accomplish in the world."
—**Thich Nhat Hanh**

I define community as a collective of folx coming together in support of a cause that they feel passionate about. Within the dynamics of community, there are typically spoken or unspoken agreements in place that allow members to feel a sense of agency, support, and collective responsibility that help them build reciprocal restorative relationships. When I think of community, I think of spaces where everyone is held with love, listened to with empathy and compassion, and viewed not as broken but as whole human beings. It is in community that we experience growth and do more together than we could as individuals. When conflict arises in this community, individuals are not written off as incapable or failures, because the community understands the complexities of personhood and uses restorative justice to repair harm between the community and the collective.

So tell me, when was the last time you felt a part of a community?

In a world that pushes individualism, where everyone is trained to be number one at any cost, focusing only on what *they* need, relationships are usually defined by their self-seeking and are rooted in selfish gain. Living in the bubble of unconscious coupling, our relationships are often shaped by their lack of boundaries in pursuit of individual need rather than collective health and well-being. Relationships can be tricky, and when those individual needs aren't met in partnership, we have two choices. One allows conflict to be the teacher and move with the energy of disruption, and the other runs away from conflict, writing people off as useless tools that no longer serve a purpose in our lives. We aren't socialized to think of relationships as sacred or communal. We're trained to throw away discomfort and uphold power over one another, dominating communication, and disappearing—either physically or emotionally—when unmet expectations reflect our childhood wound, ones we never took the time or the energy to address.

When relational expectations aren't met, we flee to protect ourselves from future wounding, and we forget that facing our wounds is what allows us to heal them. This way, when the same wound is exposed, we are present enough to actually clean them out, reviewing the past harm, doing the work to keep it from getting infected, and treating it with present-day resources, whether that be therapeutic, psychiatric, or spiritual interventions. If the goal of healing racism is to get to an individual and collective liberation, then relationships are key to moving the collective cause forward. But we can't be in whole, healed relationships with others if we haven't healed our relationship with ourselves.

Since white supremacy thrives on power, we play ourselves by seeking superficial relational connection rather than beloved community.

Like you, I have been in communities where I have both felt harm and caused harm. A majority of the harmful communities I experienced were in the Christian church. Most of my life, I knew I had a calling to serve and minister, yet every moment that I had the opportunity to show up in servant leadership, I would turn away from it and run. For years, many folx would call me Jonah, as I would be given full autonomy to lead, and instead of taking it on, I would run away. You see, throughout my church experience, I had become very biased against folx in the church. Not making space for them to be human, I held anyone in a position of authority with high esteem. When I saw parts of them that were not "Christ-like," I didn't ask questions or offer compassion, I just judged. Like most, I'd participate in the gossip Olympics that is church talk, calling out the false prophets instead of minding God's business. It took me a while to realize that such gossip was possibly the biggest danger to the community, worse than even those fallible leaders. Because when leaders aren't seen as authentic, or vulnerable, the community creates a narrative that isn't necessarily healthy.

At every opportunity I had to serve, I would run away, but then life would slap me in the face, returning me back to do what I was asked to do. But then the cycle would repeat. I would get mad at the hypocrisy of the church and once again abandon the community that I had promised to lead.

The problem was that I felt like I wasn't being seen for who I was truly was, but rather that I was being used to promote a message that the leadership wasn't upholding. After a while, I recognized that the feelings I had in the community were true, and attempts to address the issues in a restorative way were often met with pushback. I believe a person can handle resistance for only so long. Eventually, I became apathetic and walked away, knowing it was better for my mental and emotional health to leave than to continue to fight for my place in a space that did not connect with my values. I decided that I would rather find, build, and commit my efforts to a community that shared my restorative values than continue to uphold a patriarchal congregation, especially one that believed in shutting down individuals who raised concerns about the nuances of that community.

THE CONFLICT OF WHITE AMERICAN CULTURE

For the majority of our society and shared understanding of our people, white American culture (WAC) has become the dominant, unquestionable standard that we are socialized to uphold. Similar to the Invisible Knapsack of Privilege, you cannot see white culture but you always know it's there.

> Often marketed as self-reliance, being number one, and being all that you can be, WAC is the poisonous elixir that we all continue drinking until we individually choose to wake up from the stupor it produces.

It's like the story of *Snow White*, no pun intended, which is ultimately about the power dynamics of women and men, and what happens when you get sick and tired of the fuckery of systematic mistreatment.

Now I know *Snow White* is rooted in heteronormativity, patriarchy, and misogyny, but those are the lessons of white culture. Before you go dragging me for this example, remember we always have to look back at the past to make space for the present lessons on the journey.

So y'all know the story: The king meets a new woman, they fall in love and get married, the woman becomes queen and puts a spell on him. The man falls asleep to his power, which allows the queen to step into her authority, thus becoming the evil queen. The queen's magic mirror tells her she is not the most beautiful in the castle, and that Snow White, the king's daughter, is the most beautiful and the heiress to the throne. You know what happens next, right? Snow White ends up escaping the queen's "madness" and on her path ends up meeting seven little men all named after human emotions and feelings to hide her from the evil queen.

Eventually she chooses to do things her way, and the evil queen arrives, disguised as an old lady, to give her the apple. Snow White eats the apple and is put into a slumber. It isn't until Prince Charming shows up and awakens her from the spell that happily ever after is able to happen.

I might have missed some parts here, but if you take a closer look at the story, you see how it is a metaphor for white American culture—one in which matriarchy is considered a threat, patriarchy is the tool to save the day, and the only victim is the lily-white lady at its center, blameless and yet absolutely complicit in her oppression. Snow White was seen as competition and the queen didn't like it. So she tried to destroy her instead of trying to be in a shared community with her. Like white culture, many of you don't make space to see someone else's power. You see them as competition, so you figure out ways you can outperform or silence them.

The queen was so afraid of Snow's power that she was willing to put her to sleep so she wouldn't be a threat to her existence. Like any journey toward healing, you'll meet people who show you variations of this human experience. The seven little men were Snow White's opportunity to see there are multiplicities of humanity and you don't have to put yourself in a box to be seen as human. Snow White was no longer isolated, singing to birds and looking for love. She was rooted in a community who saw her for who she was and offered her an opportunity to contribute to the community in the best ways she could. In white culture, people who show variations of emotion or oddities, or who embrace the notion of community without being monolithic in their thoughts or actions, are considered cultural phenomena. The dwarves depict these unorthodox conventions. In most white cultural communities, there are unspoken rules to follow, and once you no longer follow them, you are exiled, punished, or silenced for no longer belonging to the status quo.

The real dilemma of WAC is whether you're going to eat the apple. If individuals are seen as competition, they are then denied space, because only one person can have the head seat. I am not calling you a bad white person, but I am suggesting that your behaviors are rooted in individual and systemic oppression, and until you see the relationship between white American culture and how it's reflected in your choices and how you relate to others, you will uphold white cultural standards in all areas of your life.

These standards of whiteness will inform and shape your biases and will be used to evaluate all your relationships—if someone doesn't meet or agree with your values, then you will likely not join them in relationship.

I am mixing together a few frameworks here—Judith Katz's aspects and assumptions of white culture as well as Kenneth Jones and Tema Okun's *White Supremacy Culture at Work*. When reading and looking at these perspectives, the relationship between structural and individual oppression becomes starkly clear. As we've discussed, the behaviors that are rooted in aspects and assumptions of white culture are rugged individualism, competitiveness, emotionless communication, and the Protestant work ethic.

When we look at the White Supremacy at Work framework, we see how we bring in perfectionism, sense of urgency, and the all-or-nothing thinking that is often applied to our individual ways of knowing. When you marry both frameworks, you have a society of folx who can't see beyond their comfort zones and will continue to push anyone away who does not uphold the white American culture in which they have not only been socialized but standardized.

Considering we already live in an individualistic culture, there is little focus on being in restorative relationships because we're more often focused on what we can get out of others, rather than what we can contribute. Some of you may have been lucky to have a family that taught collectivist community, but let's face it, that's a rare phenomenon in white families. The conflict of white culture is that while you are encouraged to be all that you can be, you are also encouraged to be in relationship with people just like you. If two individuals have the exact same beliefs and ideology around WAC, you will reinforce the interlocking system of oppression through the power dynamics of the relationship itself. Someone will always be the head and the other the tail. Most of white culture is heavily focused on self-reliance, winning at all costs, and muting emotions, which makes true relational interdependence almost an impossibility.

How many times have you been in a conversation with a peer and found yourself thinking of how you can one-up them with your response? You might not be thinking about it that way, but if you are preparing your answer before they finished speaking, you are working against relational interdependence. It's a subconscious choice that actually removes you from your own self-awareness because you're so focused on what you can contribute to the conversation to be more likable or more valued than the other person.

Let me say this with my whole chest: *Everyone* is socialized this way. So, don't get your panties in a bunch when I say "white culture." For me, as a Black woman who was also socialized into it, I know how the game works. I have unconsciously participated in it for my own psychological and emotional safety. Liberation from it is an ongoing practice of unfolding and becoming and allowing, as I step into the awareness of my choices, my behaviors, and my own consciousness in this world. The antiracism journey isn't about marching and reading and workshops (though that it is all part of it); it is truly about becoming conscious to our behaviors and seeing what constructs are driving our choices. Because once we are liberated from WAC, we can be truly free to be in relationship and community with one another. We can finally be freed from our own thoughts and responses, and we can deeply accept the magic of the other. We can finally decline the apple.

Unfortunately, we struggle to let go of the dominant culture because control is one of its most damaging and widely accepted myths. We are taught that we can control our destiny. However the word *control* is also closely related to power, and so when you mix the two, one must be careful to not exercise control over others. When attempting to do any soul work, it's easy to get hyperfocused on what everyone else is doing. As a white person, you can exercise power over others by coercing them to join you on your healing journey. What you aren't recognizing is how you continue to enforce white culture when demanding folx walk with you.

You can't force relationships in this work; you must allow them to unfold naturally. Your pursuit of a relationship is rooted in the fear of isolation on the journey. I get it; no one wants to do this work by themselves. It's incredibly hard, messy, and complicated. But your job isn't to control the narrative, your job is to unfold and build interdependent relationships with others, offering them the same agency and choice that we all deserve.

WELL-MODELED RELATIONSHIPS

Berkeley psychologist Dacher Keltner shares that having power makes people more likely to act like sociopaths, putting the human drive for rewards above the intimacy and connection we have with our partners.[1] This is why the power imbalances of our relationships are ever-changing. I believe that most relationships fail because the idea of shared power is not taught in oppressive systems. The current model likely trains us to be in charge, which is why softness is not seen as a gift but as a curse. You can't share power in a system that exerts power over people, which is why in an oppressive model, shared power is always a struggle, reflected to us not only in our larger community but also in our interpersonal relationships. The goal of the antiracist journey is to move into shared power, not power struggle.

As you walk this path, the invitation is to look back at your relationship to power. Consider what it means to lay down your power and interrogate what a relationship based in true intimacy and connection would look like for you. Can you imagine the joy and liberation it might offer? Do you believe you're deserving of it? Because I'll tell you right now—I'll tell me right now—you are.

DO NOW: Express gratitude. Put the book down and practice gratitude for learning and unlearning. If you'd like to take this time to create a gratitude list, write down five things for which you have been grateful to learn in this process.

For many, the notion of relationship is hard because of soul wounds attached to the past. I believe people struggle to stay in relationships because of fear of intimacy, fear of conflict, or the fear that we are not even worthy of being in a relationship. That is the work that one must continue to do, to continue interrogating our connection to relational attachment, and learning how to stay in relationships even if they are seemingly failing. This is not Myisha T Hill telling you to stay in a physically or emotionally abusive relationship. No, I am actually saying notice what comes up when you brush against reminders of the past in current relationships. Or better yet, before even getting into a relationship, take some time to do the soul work in order to understand why you may have an aversion or avoidance to the concept of relationship. When you can get to the root of your own power struggle, you will then be ready to attempt genuine relational connections and community.

THE COLLECTIVE COMMUNITY

My definition of a collectivist community and your definition of a collectivist community may be two different things. That is okay.

We live in a world where differences of opinion are rooted in binary thinking. For many of you, your journey can be delayed because you think in the context of *either/or* versus *both/and*. In this work, you must realize that the binary is at the root of our fears, leaving no space for nuance or growth. I would define a collectivist community as a group of folx who are working toward the same goal. Everyone is seen, known, and considered a valuable part of the community. In this cultural community, people are not driven by work, but by rest, joy, and pleasure. Differences are honored and respected, and the community comes together through shared agreements that allow a spaciousness of growth. At the core of this collectivist culture is restorative relationships. This collectivist community knows and understands that the work of just action requires a restorative response to harm. The community knows that there are no throwaway people and that everyone has something of value to give. To you that may seem like an abnormal and unreal experience. However, I have led a collectivist community for a while now and I have seen that this vision is possible.

> A collectivist community is held well when everyone is not forced to conform but when we are offered the chance to be ourselves, liberated and diverse, in reparative communication and justice.

Some would argue that collectivist communities are cultlike organizations, that they are dangers to society. And it's true, historically we've seen white cult leaders create communities rooted in "love" only for them to end in tragedy.

But not all communities are cults; not all collectivist models are harmful. In fact, those versions of community are usually just amplifications of interlocking systems of oppression. You can find and create a new experience of community that works for you. The system fears collectivism as a threat to their matrix. And they're right; we are. We're working as a collective to free folx from upholding the system. In fact, our goal is to disrupt it and build something new. When you begin imagining the creation of something new, the system sees it as a malfunction and will work day and night to get rid of it.

This is why collectivist communities matter. We come together and despite what it looks like, we can continue to build for social change. Notice I didn't say "fight"? Look, the "fight" has made significant progress, but there comes a time when you get tired of fighting. Building can also be tiring, but for me it brings new energy to the fatigue of the fight. Also, when we build a new system, we get to co-create what that architecture looks like. In a collectivist community, building is born from the imagination of the community and not just its leadership.

As a white person, this may sound like some superficial, spiritually bypassing bullshit. Of course for anyone who thinks intellectually, it can be hard to drop into the imagination. I am not bashing intellectualization, but if you come from a culture that rewards only intellect, imagination can feel like a foreign language. This is why many of you think that in order to have a wake-up call, one must travel to another country, indulge in other cultures, or appropriate their behaviors to help you tap into yourself. This may be true for you, but that fact is, your imagination does not require such adventures. You can also stay here in the good old USA and experience a wake-up call for radical change. You just have to choose to see, and as bell hooks would say, believe in your own capacity to be changed and transformed. As a white person you have to stop overanalyzing this work and your need to go it alone. It's a very WAC thing to think you can do it all yourself.

Outside of whiteness, most cultures have an understanding that we need one another. When whiteness came to the Americas, it normalized independence by forcing our Indigenous ancestors to socialize into white European culture. It was seen as taboo to be communal in the Indigenous ways of being and knowing. When the ancestors chose not to conform, they were named "savages" and brutally slaughtered and their land was taken. Culturally, America responded to the communal nature of the Indigenous people with a stoic independence, swinging the pendulum so far to the other side they lost whatever sense of community they might have brought with them from Europe.

Don't be that white person, the person who sees community as taboo and uses your words to slander those seeking to build a better collective for tomorrow.

> Be the white person that gets curious about community, that gets curious about the need for supporting others. Be curious to learn together, embracing curiosity to transform yourself as a member of the collective, but do not do anything in isolation.

We work in isolation because we fear intimacy, and as I mentioned in the previous chapter, you have to be willing to experience something different. Community just "hits different" as my nephew would say. You are able to see yourself in someone else's journey, making loneliness subside and bridging empathy and connection. When you are able to share your journey and walk the collective journey, it makes this work a lotta bit easier. Breaking up with American isolation is the cure that helps you finally become mentally well. If you are a person taking workshops to be better, and all you keep hearing is how bad you are for being white, that has a negative impact on your self-esteem and mental health.

Many white people I've encountered think they deserve to be treated poorly. When you have accepted systemic abuse, you will accept isolation as your path. But isolation is not the path to healing, neither yours nor mine. The fallacy of "only me" is why most mental health issues persist over time. When your mind is on the endless loop of only me, you cannot see yourself in community, but through community and peer support, you can break free of the "only me" and actually begin to heal your way forward.

I don't want to lie to you and paint the community as perfect-picture either. There's nuances to all collectives, some good and some bad. There can be a lack of consistency and interaction. There can be a fear to speak up, a fear of being seen as an outsider of shame. There can be a lot of uncertainty in the community, both on- and offline, and vulnerability can be both a threat and an incredible reward. But it's a risk one must be willing to take repeatedly to combat the isolation that the WAC consistently forces upon us. In our shame-based culture, it's hard to put your trust in others. It's the unknown that can make community terrifying.

You have to learn to trust in something that is different, and that trust takes time to build. The notion of community and relational work is hard, when we live in a world where we are constantly trying to figure out who is us or who is against us.

The goal of this work is to build beloved communities rooted in social change. When we can create and join liberated collectives, we make space for acceptance, joy, and actionable, sustainable change. There are many definitions of beloved community. bell hooks wrote, "Beloved community is formed not by the eradication of difference but *by its affirmation*, by each of us claiming the identities and cultural legacies that shape who we are and how we live in the world." Dr. King defined beloved community as, "a community where everyone is cared for, absent of poverty, hunger and hate."

When considering a co-conspired beloved community, we work with the definitions of the ancestors and elders, but we also root the work in centering the experiences of BIPOC and other marginalized persons of color. Being in co-conspired community is not centering yourself as a white person, it's about having a constant space to dismantle yourself, while showing up in action for others. It requires you to know that we are all different but we need each other for societal change. It makes space for the big feelings of this journey, but centers the work necessary for it.

As a co-conspirator, relationships are required. The gentle nudge of talking through your white ideologies is necessary to eliminate harm with someone similar to you. I am not suggesting that you work only with white folx in an affinity group. NO. I am suggesting that you get in a Black, Brown, Indigenous, Asian American, and marginalized space to learn to decenter yourself while working through the nuances of community. What this will teach you is that in intimate and connected relationship, you can go further along the journey than you ever can alone.

REFLECTION QUESTIONS ON RELATIONSHIPS

· · · · · ·

1. How were relationships modeled for you? What behaviors have you adapted in your life?

2. Are you in shared power relationships? If not, what would you like to change?

3. What does co-conspired relationships look like to you? Do you need more of them?

· 10 ·

A REPARATIVE FUTURE

"Help us to be ever faithful gardeners of the spirit,
who know that without darkness nothing comes to
birth, and without light nothing flowers."
—May Sarton

I f you looked only at the external world, it would seem as though we're walking through a daily shitshow of the unknown. Media is constantly bombarding us with messages that dysregulate our nervous systems, keeping us in constant states of flight, fight, or freeze. Our interpersonal relationships can feel like a constant push and pull with no direction and no give, while our lives can feel like the Bill Murray movie *Groundhog Day*. You wake up to life events every day, hoping something will be different, only realizing that life is on repeat. You crave radical change, peace of mind, and substance only to find more fear, drama, and insecurity. But like Bill's character in the movie, eventually you see a way to turn life's repetitive cycle into your own adventure. That's the joy of the journey, waking up and realizing you get to choose what anti-oppression, abolition, and liberation look and feel like for you. And then you get to feel your way into being a part of the greater collective moving toward freedom.

By now, you know that the system is working exactly the way it's supposed to. Many would say it's broken, but after seeing my ancestors fight to the death to fix it, only to have Supreme Courts, governments, and policies continue to tear down their work, I can say, it isn't broken; it's working exactly as it was intended. I am not saying don't advocate for policies and systemic change; what I am suggesting is that we speak up for our rights while working in tandem to collectively focus on repairing ourselves, nurture meaningful relationships, and restore humanity's call to justice.

> When we reimagine collective liberation, we can build sustainable change, which is why integration of the head, heart, and hands is critical for this work to be nuanced and whole.

There are limitless possibilities when it comes to repairing the future, and we get to choose what that co-creation looks like. As a co-conspirator, you co-create by trusting BIPOC, marginalized, LGBTQ+, and disabled folx to guide you, centering our lived experiences toward collective healing and liberation. So where do we go from here? What is a reparative future? *Repair* is defined as meaning to fix or mend something, and since none of us are broken, we need to accept the invitation into lifelong healing. Healing isn't linear and so we must first look inside ourselves and unsettle the thoughts, behaviors, and actions that replicate systemic, interpersonal, and individual oppression. If you aren't sure how you are upholding the system, I invite you to look at your relationships with your children, your partner, and even your work colleagues. Those are the greatest mirrors of how you are replicating harm in your life.

I didn't know I was upholding the interlocking systems of oppression until I recognized that my addiction to overworking and performing was causing harm to my family. Distraction is a tool of supremacy, and my addiction to my smartphone kept me from being 100 percent in tune with myself and my family. When the Great White Awakening happened, the addiction got real. I had already begun the addiction prior to the awakening, when I first began working from home as an entrepreneur and for my previous employer. But the awakening amplified and enhanced that disorder into a full-blown illness.

I can't count how many times within the last year my family begged me to put my phone down and attune to them. I was so distracted with leading "the work" that I was no longer practicing presence, or caring about the needs of my family. I was in first class on the capitalist supremacy train of success. Zoom calls, IG Lives, courses, speaking engagements, and program launches became the norm. Family time was filled with me doomscrolling to zone out, to not be present to the people who needed me most. I was so distracted by capitalism that even when I spent ninety days fighting with repetitive stress headaches and panic attacks, I continued to perform and push my family away, upholding WAC's demands for perfection and sense of urgency. I worked myself to the bone even on vacation, making sure that I was still the main attraction.

As I grew more and more addicted to capitalist success, my family became emotionally numb and distant. Not only was I wrestling with an addiction to my phone, work, and business, I was also upholding this overwhelming system of digital oppression. I wasn't listening to the needs of "my people." Sure, I was working to make sure that they had their basic needs met (an easy argument for anyone who has mouths to feed), but I wasn't present to the spectrum of social, mental, and emotional needs to support building a *healthy* family community. Notice the first four letters in *healthy* are *heal*? We'll come back to that.

It was not until I experienced a series of family emergencies that I remembered that pain and discomfort are our greatest teachers. I began to recognize that I was addicted to the imperialist, capitalist, white supremacist patriarchy. Imperialist thinking had me exercise my authority to make excuses as to why I couldn't attune to the people I loved most, instead gaslighting them to just deal with it. Capitalism allowed me to buy their time with toys and gadgets. Ableist thinking had me forget their neurodivergence, assuming that they were able-bodied enough to figure shit out on their own. The white gaze of supremacist patriarchy had me feeling like I was an exceptional Black person, and kept me distracted from paying attention to the emotional needs of my family. I felt a heightened sense of esteem 'cause white folx put me on a pedestal for having a voice. In response, I unconsciously reinforced and replicated the system's oppression by disregarding my family's needs and my own boundaries in return for blue checks and paychecks. But here is the thing, once I became aware of this, I decided to reverse my course. I started to make choices to guide myself and my family toward a reparative future.

Again, this journey isn't linear. We are going to have challenges, obstacles, and "failures," or rather, lessons for growth. For me, my newfound awareness took me on a journey similar to the co-conspirator's journey, moving with shame, recommitting, asking for repair, and working to be in a continued state of awareness and self-authenticity. And likewise, repairing myself and my relationships has not been a linear process. I'd be lying if I said I have fixed everything—we cannot fix ourselves overnight.

However, I can practice healing this stuff by engaging in rituals of restorative care that put my spiritual life first, my family, second, and my career, third. It isn't perfect, but often it's the messy middle that keeps us pressing toward the mark of justice for all.

My hope is that as a white person reading this, you can see yourself in my story. I am not sharing my struggle with white supremacy so you feel sorry for me. Even feeling sorry for me is rooted in white saviorism. I share my story for our common humanity, so you can see yourself and find your way through your own journey. The journey of repair is an ongoing process. In restorative circles, the goal isn't to fix anything overnight.

Depending on the situation, the goal is to keep the community together to allow individuals within the collective to be seen and heard in hopes of reducing harm and hopefully integrating them back into community.

> In restorative practice, we don't throw anyone
> away for causing harm, we connect them
> back into community in order to transform
> their hurt into healing.

In this work, I envision repair as an ongoing restorative process, constantly inviting us to engage in practices not rooted in selfish ambition, but abolition, anti-oppression, and building a legacy of love for future generations. This vision includes the practice of community, facilitation of reparations, mutual aid, and emotional and financial security for BIPOC. For you as a white person, a reparative future should be dealing with the wounds of the past rather than seeking quick solutions from one-day workshops. A reparative future engages in education, but commits to community and mutual respect.

PLANTING SEEDS FOR A REPARATIVE FUTURE

Your reparative future isn't about power hoarding and consuming; it's about engaging more with spirit and soul connectedness. It's about embodying more joy, more pleasure, more giving, more passion, and less ownership. For you, repair is ultimately about participation in reparations; it's about speaking up and decentering yourself. Your reparative future is the invitation to walk through the valley of the shadow of death, and then to return to those shadows over and over again. As you enter and continue on this journey, the massive amount of new information you receive can be exciting, painful, and often overwhelming. It will take a long time of doing this work, rooted in community, witnessing yourself through the eyes of others, to begin to integrate the head, heart, and hands.

As I mentioned, "whiteness cannot see outside of itself," a quote from my friend Louiza Doran, which according to her means, "White people are socialized to not see how whiteness functions in order for the system to maintain itself. You cannot address what you can't see, and the system continues to update itself." As a white or white-passing person, your limited understanding of how the world works will be challenged, positioning you in the messy middle. From that space, you will be forced to choose between constant discomfort or aversion. As a white person at any moment of this work, you can avoid knowledge of your collusion with oppression by constantly averting your eyes from what's obvious, distracting yourself with screen time, consumption, and all the pretty shiny things that keep you uneasy but kinda comfortable. Or you can lean into the enormous discomfort of seeing injustice and asking yourself, *What's my part in all this?* The invitation for repair is to step outside your comfort zone and stretch into what feels uncomfortable. It's not about love and light but rather about embracing the shadows, embracing *your* shadow, and moving that energy to do good in the world. Your reparative future is the foundation for your ongoing journey of healing. You get to choose, and my hope is that you choose to heal your way forward.

DO NOW: Dance. If you've been reading for at least fifteen minutes, take time to connect to your body. One of the easiest ways to do this is to turn to the "Heal Your Way Forward" playlist on Spotify and move your body to the music. Be sure to set a five-minute timer so you can get back to what you were doing.

The work of a reparative future is calling you to get rid of the tools that no longer serve you, those well-worn tools of white supremacy. Instead, it is offering you a new tool belt to pick up the gardening kit of liberation and ground yourself as you plant new seeds for the future. Since we are building a new legacy, we must walk a new path, one rooted in purpose, hope, abolition, transformative justice, liberation, community, and restorative relationship.

REDEFINING THE WORK

There is a time and season for everything. I believe we are in the pruning stage of oppression. We have been awakened to heal forward, and the only way is to repair ourselves in order to move from movement fighting into legacy building. A new legacy will allow us to envision a world in which we can develop new ideologies and practices and build sustainable change. I believe transformative justice is at the root of our reparative future.

We have a new responsibility to heal ourselves, but this new reparative version of healing cannot be accomplished through the old constructs. Instead, it requires a new understanding of what it means to heal. Since language is political, be open to having things defined by the constructs that will and should shape this new future—abolition, anti-oppression, restorative justice, and the end of throwaway culture. We cannot continue to use a one-size-fits-all approach to language, and in this work, each scholar, guide, or leader will use definitions that connect to their work. There are multiple meanings for language in an anti-oppressive practice. I am sharing my definitions of abolition, anti-oppression, transformative justice, and throwaway culture as a guide, leaving space for you to cultivate a practice that works on your journey.

"People do abolition every day when they connect to their community, learn how to take accountability, and foster communal responsibility for preventing and responding to harm."[1] Abolitionists are folx who work for the abolishment of harmful practices due to structural or institutional oppression. When it comes to the word *abolitionist*, many of us think of those who fought for the end of enslavement. Abolition can be seen today as activist work to end the prison-industrial complex, or the special education-industrial complex. As a practice, abolition consists of building new systems in order to replace the systemically racist structures that have been replicated over time. As a gardener in this work, you must be willing to abolish systems or policies that are harmful. It's not a one-and-done practice. We are weeding out the old, and like most weeds, systemic racism is intrusive and always working to regrow itself, sometimes in obvious ways, other times, in ways that are far subtler.

The oppressed, having internalized the image of the oppressor and adopted his guidelines, are fearful of freedom. There are hella definitions of oppression, but I like to borrow a definition from *The Social Work Dictionary*, edited by Robert L. Barker:

> The social act of placing severe restrictions on an individual, group or institution. Typically, a government or political organization that is in power places these restrictions formally or covertly on oppressed groups so that they may be exploited and less able to compete with other social groups. The oppressed individual or group is devalued, exploited and deprived of privileges by the individual or group which has more power.

Anti-oppression is the practice of moving away from devaluation and exploitation in both your individual and interpersonal relationships as well as at institutional and structural levels. The seed of anti-oppression is one that requires daily watering, as oppression is embedded in all of us, in our systems and structures. But once you see it, you cannot unsee it.

In order to build toward a reparative future, your work is to not only sustainably move away from participating in it, but to dismantle it. This is the daily practice of antiracism.

Marginalized communities have practiced transformative justice for generations, planting the seeds of this work as a

communal response to the interlocking systems of oppression. According to author and transformative justice educator Mia Mingus:

> Transformative Justice (TJ) is a political framework and approach for responding to violence, harm and abuse. At its most basic, it seeks to respond to violence without creating more violence and/or engaging in harm reduction to lessen the violence. TJ can be thought of as a way of "making things right," getting in "right relation," or creating justice together. Transformative justice responses and interventions 1) do not rely on the state (e.g. police, prisons, the criminal legal system, I.C.E., foster care system) though some TJ responses do rely on or incorporate social services like counseling; 2) do not reinforce or perpetuate violence such as oppressive norms or vigilantism; and most importantly, 3) actively cultivate the things we know prevent violence such as healing, accountability, resilience, and safety for all involved.

Like most social frameworks, transformative justice shouldn't be used as another buzz word to throw around at the white woke Olympics. No, we must apply transformative justice with the intention and commitment of gardeners planting new seeds toward a better tomorrow. In practice this looks like living into the work. When you live into the work, there is a spaciousness that allows you to move with the flow, and not against it.

Throwaway culture, or callout culture, is the practice of using shame to bring someone into awareness of their wrongs. Typically what happens is folx shame each other for not behaving correctly and gaslight folx into silence, throwing them away for not upholding norms of behavior. I don't think folx recognize this as upholding white supremacy patriarchy. Ending throwaway culture is a seed that needs cultivation time and time again.

Patriarchy shames and silences us when we no longer uphold its rules and regulations. We see this all the time in the workplace. Individuals who hold companies accountable for their harmful policies are disruptors who are tired of unethical practices in the workplace. They are people who bring attention to issues within the current constructs and are often silenced or shamed for speaking their truth. They are "disruptors" for not following the status quo. How many times have you seen people at worked shamed for calling out corporate harm? They are often isolated and forced out when companies begin to track their behavior and warn colleagues about their behavior. This shame-based practice is rooted in oppression and does more harm than good.

Like gardeners, we must be in tune with the seasons of life in order to support the growth of each seed planted. They will need to be watered, planted, harvested, and composted over and over again. Time is critical, which is why we must work in alignment with others to make sure their gardens are also growing toward a new legacy. This means getting proximate with people who don't look like you, supporting their progress in their garden. Getting proximate is getting close to white folx who are from the same socioeconomic class as you, with the hopes that they might change. Proximity means going to the south side of Chicago known as the "low-end" and planting your garden next to someone else's, giving your supplies in hopes of helping their garden grow. It's not about you just showing up and sowing seeds, it's about building relationships on the communities' terms in support of their growth and evolution.

In *Check Your Privilege*, Jennifer Kinney shares, "When I became proximate to the global majority, the complexity and reality of this history came to life through the people around me, I realized how ignorant I had been. These realizations propelled me into studying history more. I have learned a lot about what it looks like to live into the work. I have been listening and learning from Black educators and am developing the language I need to understand racism and better engage dialogue. Focusing primarily on my internal work over the last several years has allowed me to observe, learn, and deconstruct a lot of the subtle racist messaging I had consumed growing up as a white woman in the U.S."

> **Proximity is not about rescuing or saving, it's living out history, stepping back and showing up in solidarity as you evolve in your own work. Remember, each garden is there to support the ecosystem of the greater, more liberated collective.**

When you witness yourself as a planter in the garden of liberation, you are able to witness others in the community in process with you. You recognize that your garden is not greener than your neighbor's, but rather that it works in tandem with theirs, cultivating a legacy of root work, reaping, harvesting, and replanting. There are seeds of commitment, reparations, mutual aid, and community that are necessary to cultivate a reparative future.

ACTIONS FOR THE JOURNEY AHEAD

Your participation in mutual aid, reparations, and Indigenous sovereignty are just three ways to participate in reparative action. Many of you get stuck or overwhelmed with these concepts, but they are important to help those of us from the global majority heal from the systemic, interpersonal, and intergenerational harm we have experienced within the interlocking systems of oppression.

Mutual aid is a practice of redistributing your resources by bypassing the system's participation in distributing those resources. While both practices are anti-oppressive and anti-colonial, it's a long-term commitment to support communities with resources to help sustain them. Some folx like to argue that the practice of mutual aid is exclusive to rich white men with elite status. While that may be true (i.e., legacy admissions to universities), historically, mutual aid networks were cultivated in communities of color. In the 1800s, Black mutual aid societies existed where free Black Americans gathered their resources together to provide land and farms to take care of women and children. In Asian cultures, lending circles, called *hui*, are often used to pool money for medicine, houses, cars, and burial expenses. Mutual aid was the process of cultural communities coming together to support one another against oppressive regimes that provided them with no support. As you engage in the practice of mutual aid, rather than worrying about where the money is really going, consider looking at the impact your resources will have on those who need access to what you have. It is a privilege, no pun intended, to sit back and not participate when mutual aid is called upon.[2]

Another reparative action you can take is participation in, well, reparations. Now, as similar as they might sound, let me remind you that mutual aid is not reparations. Reparations are the practice of making amends for a wrong one has been done, by paying money, or to otherwise help those who have been wronged. African Americans are the only racial group in America that has not been offered reparations for our contributions to society. In fact, the United States has given more money to other victims of atrocities, than those who are still dealing with the legacy of enslavement. As a Black American, I am constantly enraged by the lack of reparations to my people. It just makes common sense, but what else can we expect from a nation that thrives in anti-Blackness and continues to treat Black people like a commodity?

The commodification of the Black body is nothing more than a useful tool of the larger oppression by white American culture. There is no other culture with the same legacy of enslavement that has been trained to accept the constant mistreatment and exploitation of our lives and human experience. America should be ashamed of itself, and *you* should be ashamed of America. Being ashamed of America is not a challenge to your civil liberties; it's a wake up to call leadership into alignment with what is right. I was seven years old when reparation resolutions were first presented to Congress. In 1989, Rep. John Conyers introduced HR 40, which would create a commission to study the impact of slavery and make proposals for reparations to descendants of millions of enslaved Africans. Spoiler: It never passed.

In 2021, thirty-nine-year-old congresswoman Rep. Sheila Johnson reintroduced the bill, and currently a House committee has voted to move forward with it, establishing a commission to develop proposals to help repair the lasting effects of slavery. If you're reading this and you think this is a step in the right direction, it may be. I won't hold my breath, because much like the

George Floyd Justice and Policing Act, which was voted against, I have a strong feeling that this will not be resolved in my generation. My grandchildren may be the ones who make this law a reality, but that doesn't mean we *stop* advocating for reparations in the present. This is your invitation to take action in your own life and local communities to push reparations forward. Make it a practice to give 10 percent of your income to community Black-led local or online initiatives supporting better health outcomes, mental health initiatives, and generational wealth for Black folx.

Don't get caught up in the politics of giving. If you believe that *Black Lives Matter*, then you have a responsibility to support the movement for reparations.

Ta-Nehisi Coates has a beautiful article in *The Atlantic* entitled "The Case for Reparations," that I recommend you read to unpack the historical legacy of Black trauma and how reparations helps Black communities move forward toward healing.

When considering taking action for our Indigenous siblings, we must consider the legacy of manifest destiny, land theft, native American boarding schools, and deliberate genocide. Your responsibility to our Indigenous siblings is the investment in Indigenous Sovereignty.

This practice is distinguishable from Tribal Sovereignty in that it is not a nation-state recognition of inherent sovereignty under nation-state dominion. Rather, it arises from Indigenous Traditional Knowledge, belonging to each Indigenous nation, tribe, first nation, community, etc. It consists of spiritual ways, culture, language, social and legal systems, political structures, and inherent relationships with lands, waters and all upon them. Indigenous sovereignty exists regardless of what the nation-state does or does not do. It continues as long as the People that are a part of it continue.[3]

As a white person, you can begin practicing Indigenous sovereignty by participating in the ritual of land reverence, rent relief funds, land reclamation funds, and Indigenous educator support. And lastly, support Indigenous peoples and culture but do not appropriate their culture. With land reverence being a free ritual, I challenge you to invest in learning the history of the Indigenous tribe whose land you have occupied, connecting into the community to learn how to be a better co-conspirator for their communal hearing.

This reparative action list is not inclusive and does not count initiatives to support our disabled, LGBTQ+, AAPI, or Latinx siblings. I want to challenge you to get proximate to the issues that affect all of us and the ways you can support our collective work toward healing and liberation.

Healing your way forward is about not just looking at the light of your journey, but also your shadow. It encourages you to work through your unseen spaces and knowing to reconcile with yourself, moving into interdependent boundaries for accountability and support. The co-conspirator's journey is not one rooted in isolation or spiritual bypassing, nor is it about forgetting or papering-over; this work is about facing yourself, unsettling and reckoning the past to heal seven generations forward.

It's a journey of moving with shame, becoming more loving and less judging, and connecting into self-compassion and forgiveness. This work is honoring your humanity just as you understand that it is tied to mine. Most importantly, this work is giving yourself the grace to get shit wrong and try all over again. Remember, none of us really know what we're doing, but as we heal the wounds of the past, we move toward the reparative future our children and our children's children deserve to see realized.

REFLECTION QUESTIONS ON
A REPARATIVE FUTURE

· · · · · ·

1. What is the interconnection of transformative justice, anti-oppression, and abolition on your healing journey?

2. How can you participate in giving reparations, mutual aid, or participate in the act of Indigenous sovereignty?

3. How will you move from compartmentalizing the work to embodying the experience of the work in your life? What does a reparative future look like for you?

CONCLUSION

"You are responsible for your life. You can't keep
blaming somebody else for your dysfunction. Life is
really about moving on."
—Oprah Winfrey

The co-conspirator's journey is a process that requires us to
cultivate gardens of change, adapting with the seasons and
the cycles of life change. When cultivating, composting, and harvesting ourselves on the journey forward, you must be able to
notice the nuances of the path.

I don't have all the answers, but what I've learned is that healing is really about taking responsibility for your life. No one is
coming to save you or fix you, so it's up to you to move your life
forward and let go of the systemic dysfunctions that have held us
back. Every moment we choose to remain unhealed, we are
choosing a self-imposed prison of oppression. The system thrives
on us living as prisoners to it. In turn, we unconsciously perpetuate it in ourselves and project it onto others. But it's easier to
blame someone else for our own hurts, habits, and hang-ups than
to focus on liberation. We blame our parents, school teachers, the

left or right, but while we are pointing fingers outside of ourselves, we allow fear, self-sabotage, and lack of self-love to keep us from living and being fully liberated people.

Like you, I am also on the rocky path toward liberation. As a highly sensitive person, I see and sense the world with a heightened state of self-awareness. As I discussed, a highly sensitive person is someone with an increased central nervous system response to physical, emotional, or social stimuli. Not being verbally expressive as a child created a fractured sense of self, but through the lifelong journey of finding myself, I discovered that the only way I could begin to liberate myself was to find out what I loved.

I used to care a lot about what everybody thought of me; when I heard the word "no," I would withdraw and grow inward. For those of us growing up under the contrasts of oppression, it was a sin to have your own opinion. I was passive and not direct. Most of us fear saying the wrong thing rather than meaning what we say and saying what we mean. Outside of having an expressive communication delay, it was hard for me to speak without having folx guess, unscramble, and translate my words. I was living out of fear and low self-esteem rather than being rooted in love, joy, and boldness.

I am not sure how long you have been on the journey of becoming, but if you've been compartmentalizing antiracism work as just another chore you have to do, you are not taking responsibility for the whole experience of mind-body-heart healing. In my opinion, compartmentalization is a consequence of being afraid of how we will be received or perceived by our peers. It's easy for us to jump on bandwagon movements that perpetuate bandwagon fallacy because we fear what other people might think of our personal journey. The bandwagon fallacy is all about getting people to do or think something because "everyone else is doing it" or "everything else thinks this."[1] Rather than engaging in meaningful healing work, most folx jump on initiatives and movements because our heart gets pulled into trauma porn and quick fixes rather than ongoing solutions. Taking responsibility for your journey means you jump off the bandwagon and stop compartmentalizing the work.

You don't know what you don't know, *and* even after reading this book, you still may not know what you're doing, but as long as you are actively practicing and unfolding, you are in your healing work. Unfortunately, we often seek out standard operating procedures for living, but the only way to know what procedures work for you is to break free from oppression and co-create your own. If you have been operating under the lens of oppression, dominating conversations, co-opting movements, and expressing power over folx, those behaviors are not in service to you anymore.

As we grow through what we go through, the healing journey becomes a sustainable cycle of trusting the unknown. You know your own path forward when honoring your commitments to yourself, trusting the nuances of community connection, and grounding yourself in the messy middle on the path to healing your way forward.

HONORING OUR COMMITMENTS

In life, we are always on a hamster wheel of our to-do list, which distracts us from committing to the journey. Because the truth is we do have time to practice consistency. But you cannot be committed to something if you're choosing not to be consistent with it. It is a practice. Just like going to a 9-to-5 job is a consistent daily practice. Your alarm goes off, you wake up, get in the shower, eat breakfast, go to work, do all this work for somebody else for eight hours, come home, do family stuff if you have family, cook dinner, watch TV or read a book or listen to a podcast, and go to bed. It is a ritual, or rather like the movie *Groundhog Day*, where you commit to a repetition but not necessarily the thing that creates sustainable change.

The sad part is we are more committed to going to a 9-to-5 that likely upholds systemic oppression than committing to healing the things in ourselves that are causing harm from the same 9-to-5 in any other aspect of your life. The way that 9-to-5 treats you is the way that you treat yourself, which is why you replicate systems of harms on other people. If you feel oppressed at work, you probably also feel oppressed in your personal life. So commitment to anything that helps you feel liberated is abnormal and not a part of this status quo.

It's hard to be committed to a journey that feels isolating, overwhelming, and sometimes daunting. If you aren't committed, though, how can you stay actively engaged in your healing process? What does commitment even mean to you? I'd like to offer that commitment is a practice of being dedicated to a person, project, or process that honors my needs to feel whole and human. When talking to my partner Mario Ruiz, I asked him, why aren't people committed to the process? He said, "It's probably a lack of information, engagement, and an issue with their surroundings and interest level." It reminds me that all of our healing journeys need to be intentional, intriguing, and engaging. Most humans cannot be part of a process that doesn't feel genuine, humble, fun, or connected. I believe we aren't committed because we do not know what we want and/or we have not been taught what commitment really looks like. Culturally speaking, all cultures think commitments are different, but if commitment is about interconnection, then our values must be aligned.

When choosing to be committed to this work, we must all begin to release the stories of victimhood that keep us from being fully engaged. Victimhood is a personality trait that we adopt based on how people treat us or behave toward us. Healing forward means we are taking responsibility for seeing ourselves outside the constructs of oppression. Even if we feel like a victim, we get to choose to stand in our personal power and refuse to allow victimhood to stop our movement toward self and collective liberation.

Moving out of victimhood means we are able to move into self-compassion and vulnerability. In dominant culture, self-compassion is equated with selfishness, but it isn't selfish to do what you need to do to take care of yourself.

Self-compassion is the practice of treating yourself as you would treat a friend. It's the practice of honoring your struggles not through judgment but through recognizing that your self-perceived failures are just part of the human experience.

As Buddhist monk Thich Nhat Hanh writes, "When I understand my suffering, I love myself, and I know how not to keep nourishing the suffering, how to transform the suffering. I get lighter, I become more compassionate, and with that kind of freedom and compassion, I feel liberated." When you see your human experience as the practice of self-love, vulnerability is no longer taboo. Even though the dominant culture still struggles to see its importance, the global majority is normalizing it in practice.

Without the practice of vulnerability, we lean into fear and detach from our commitments. As Brené Brown, the vulnerability guru herself, shares, "Our willingness to own and engage with our vulnerability determines the depth of our courage and the clarity of our purpose; the level to which we protect ourselves from being vulnerable is a measure of our fear and disconnection."

Choosing to engage with vulnerability is allowing ourselves the opportunity to engage in the work in a more meaningful way. When we move into vulnerability, we feel more connected to the process and our commitments can be honored. Vulnerability allows you to accept and drop into the nuance of this lifelong journey, allowing you to say "I will commit to my healing" as well as "It's okay to give up when I am tired."

Vulnerability allows us to practice self-compassion to see self-perceived failure as the stepping stones to greater change. We can fully commit to this process by accepting that we are imperfect beings striving to be better first for ourselves and, second, for the collective. Because if you are constantly putting yourself last, you will burn out and not return. Commitment on this journey is the practice of self-acceptance, niching down our journey and moving from scarcity to sustainability by trusting the messy middle of the work.

TRUSTING THE MESSY MIDDLE

Living into the work is essentially a journey into mindfulness. When you're living with this every moment of every day, it becomes a life journey of mindfulness, self-awareness, compassion, and accepting the mess. When you accept, you stay in constant awareness of the work. In the Co-Conspirator's Lounge, we have this golden agreement to "lean into the tension of non-closure, to expect and accept it because the work is never done and we may not get to a resolution. However, we can reduce the harm we cause to ourselves and others."

We know that we can create change and yet we have to accept when change does not take place the way we want it to. When we stay in a binary of truth, we limit our ability to see things from a different perspective. On this journey, we must be willing to learn how to make space for multiple truths. It is not our job to convert everyone to be on Team Justice, but when we hold space for multiple differences, we can begin to be flexible in the way we process and practice the journey ahead.

As author and facilitator Craig Freshly offers, "It is very rare for any two or more people to agree that a certain thing happened exactly the same way or for exactly the same reasons. How things look always depends on where one sits and no two people have the same perspective." Being in the messy middle means you don't necessarily have to see things exactly the same, but you can have similarities in perspective that may support greater understanding. In a world where everyone is fighting to be right, the messy middle gives space where we can consider, though not necessarily agree, with another perspective.

Truth and multiple truths can be seen as a complex topic. When making space for healing and reconciliation, I am reminded of the four truths model created by the Truth and Reconciliation Commission (TRC) of South Africa during the abolition of apartheid in the 1990s.

The four truths were:

1. **Forensic Truth:** The familiar legal or scientific notion of bringing to light factual, corroborated evidence, of obtaining accurate information through reliable sources.

2. **Personal Truth:** This is the truth of personal recollection and memory—the world as viewed from one perspective. It is the product of personal experience and a selected subset of forensic evidence.

3. **Social Truth**: This is a truth constructed from multiple personal narratives interacting with each other—either agreed upon by society as a whole or a subset of society. Oftentimes social truths will clash when held by different identity and affinity groups.

4. **Reconciliatory Truth**: Sometimes also called the "Public Truth," this is the process of exposing conflicting or disparate Personal and Social Truths to each other and working toward a shared understanding and conclusion from their meanings.

Somewhere in the messy middle is the space to embody these four truths as we move into defining collective liberation for all. Wouldn't it be great to have a deeper understanding of personal truth versus collective truth? We know that systems of oppression embody domination and power *over*, so room for multiple truths isn't taught. As we begin to trust nuance and messiness, we make space to allow the middle to be a place of uncharted territory that helps us to lean into our discomfort and trust the unknown.

The unknown is a scary place when you are used to thinking in the binary. On this journey, you must be willing to let life be the teacher. Life experiences are an asset, and we are all students of their lessons. When we allow life to lead, we can make space for allowing. Allowing things to happen without the need to control anything outside of ourselves is a constant practice of unfolding, of letting go so we have the space to receive the messages needed to grow on our journey. This is the co-conspirator's journey, one that allows for nuance of humanness, humanity, and trusting the messy middle and complexities of life.

THE CO-CONSPIRATOR'S JOURNEY
AS A WAY OF LIFE

I often use the catchphrase "Just live." It's a phrase that reminds me to live like there is no tomorrow. To experience life unapologetically, to encounter my full human self *as* whole, lacking nothing, accepting that *I am* who I say I am, not what society determines me to be. Just living is an active state of aliveness, a practice of honoring presence. And that presence is the process of being fully aware, removing the distractions that stop me from being in this moment. That includes monitoring my social media usage, and any other tools that distract me from being fully present for myself and family. When it comes to antiracism work, "Just live" essentially means get out of the practice of just doing things for the sake of saying it's done. We need to just live into the work—making it alive and aware in all of our choices, behaviors, and ideologies.

There was a season when most of us in the justice space told folx to just do something, without any explanation of what that something was and how to approach it. I believe that the catchphrase "Do the work" set people up on another colonialist quest of proving they are good by their virtuous actions. Doing does not equate to living an experience. It pushes you into action, but it also begins to feel like another mundane task on a never-ending to-do list. In reality, anyone can take a workshop or teach a workshop, give calls to actions, and do what feels good at any moment. But we can't *be* less of anything until we begin to *live* into the experience ourselves.

Living into the work gives space to practice this work authentically and somatically in relation to self and with others. It allows us to name our experience in shared space, while also working toward creating a better tomorrow. Living into the work means you can authentically show up, not with your preconceived notions but as a lifelong learner willing to empty your mind and allow yourself to be shaped beyond your conditioned experience. You practice living into the work by allowing every point of the co-conspirator's journey to be an ongoing lesson toward liberation. Every journey is also different for everyone according to age and ability, so what works for you on this journey may not work for someone else, and that's okay, too. Make space to allow folx the grace to not be like you. None of us are monoliths, and when we make space for someone else's path and not try to force them on ours, we allow healing to take place for everyone . . . at their own pace.

Each part of this journey heals a part of your life that you likely never recognized needed healing. Sometimes each part of this journey will repeat itself until the lessons are learned. For many of us, those lessons aren't picked up the first time; it may even take a lifetime. But a lifetime of trust in the work is what guides us to creating paths for the generations behind us to walk upon.

I like to think of the generation before us as the ones who mixed the cement, but our job is to pour the pavement to allow a solid foundation for the next iteration of healers, scholars, politicians, game-changers, and influencers. Our job is twofold, to heal our wounds in order to heal the collective intergenerational trauma. Know this: The path forward isn't the easiest. But the co-conspirator's journey is a multidimensional approach to healing your relationship with individual oppression and systemic oppression; while one step works in tandem with others, this journey helps us heal our way forward.

THE PRACTICE

I call this journey a practice because on your path you will be met with obstacles. In the age of COVID, and even prior, quick fixes and solutions do not work anymore. We must constantly be prepared to see life swing its pendulums. Understanding this allows us to see practice not as a pathway to perfection but as an ongoing effort to humanize our life experiences. Let's take a look at the steps of the journey to remind ourselves of the practices ahead.

AWAKENING

The awakening phase on the journey will be a constant reminder of why you started the journey in the first place. Many folx who came into the work in 2020 used the attack in January 2021 as a reason to see themselves as an exceptional white person because they were "antiracist." If that was you, you still have more work to do, because you are not an exception. None of us are. That type of othering doesn't allow us to heal anything. When we are in awakening, we are always noticing, not from judgment, but from spaces of inquiry. Inquiry keeps us curious, asking ourselves, *What is this inviting me to know right now . . . about myself?* This may take you back on the spiral of shame, and that's okay, because grief comes behind every awakening process.

GRIEF

Grief is the teacher and we are the students. When coming into this work, it's important to make space for your grief. If we aren't making conscious and deliberate space for grief, then we will be always centering ourselves and our needs versus being able to be of service to the community. For every moment of injustice, you must grieve before you act, otherwise you're performing and moving like a machine. One of the practices we have in our community is to wait twenty-four hours to process before we move into radical action. It allows us time to cry, hold a circle, name the injustice(s), and come back to work another day. We get to move out of hyperproductivity and drop into our hearts first before we move forward with our heads and hands. Feeling our grief is how we move forward in humanity. If anyone tells you you can't feel in this work, then it's time for you to find some new folx with which to be in community. The grief process allows us to listen, to make space for others to share their hearts.

LISTENING

As Jimi Hendrix once wrote, "Knowledge speaks, but wisdom listens." Most of us don't listen to understand, but rather to defend or to fix. We lack the ability to sit with the discomfort of other people's feelings, and so we minimize what they say to prove we know what's best for them. In the justice world, a lot of well-meaning white folx are working from a savior's agenda. People aren't broken and your job isn't to fix anyone. Your job is to listen with compassion, to allow someone the space to be seen as fully human. You're listening to get to the roots but not to pull them up. Listening isn't about how much information you obtain to prove you're woke; it is the practice of learning, of gathering information to inform what specific sustainable action looks like on your journey.

LEARNING

Learning is where listening and imagination meet. When you understand your learning style and how you process information, taking action can seem like a walk in the park. Learning encompasses compassion, asking questions, and understanding yourself. It is understanding both the integrity within the process and the personal integrity of your values and acting in alignment with them. It is really important that the process in which you are engaged reflects your values. Striving to be open, to stay curious, and to compassionately understand other people's viewpoints and feelings help build empathy. Compassion and empathy are what allow us to take action without harm. When you recognize the journey is constant unlearning and relearning, you can see action as the constant teacher that shapes your next step forward…or even backward.

ACTION

Just because you take action doesn't mean you perfect the journey ahead. Hate to break it to you, but you are not the superhero for the global majority. Any notion of perfectionism is rooted in colonial thinking, stopping us from living as full humans and instead putting us back on the workhorse of productivity, doing things for the sake of saying they are done. Action requires empathy, reflection, and knowing what saviorism looks like within you. You must be careful to do all you need to do to understand your intentions and the impact they may have on someone else. Be careful that you are not trying to caretake. You have to know that your assignment is not about fixing or rescuing. It's using your privilege to do good and to ask the global majority (BIPOC) what we need.

Taking action without checking in with your heart can be a dangerous practice. It's easy to intellectualize this work thinking we know, but we don't know until we ask. Action requires empathetically asking people what they need, not making assumptions because of what we think we know. That is where this work becomes dangerous, when we know everything. It's better to come in with a beginner's mind, knowing there are many ways to take action. You have to know where you fit in the movement; not everyone is meant to be front and center. By recognizing your place, you will better understand that the action is deeper than a quick fix, going beyond fear and shame and into the vulnerability of communal need.

SHAME AND VULNERABILITY

Shame is the teacher; you are not the shame. When you can embrace shame as a teacher and not attach it to yourself as part of your personality, you can move through the nuances of shame versus spiraling downward into it. We live in a shame culture and are used to being seen as a problem. We know this is true because compliments feel odd when we aren't readily willing to accept them. We flog our sense of praise because we are so used to tearing ourselves down thanks to the constructs of success and perfectionism. When we can look at shame not as who we are but as the reminder of who we aren't, we can move into the vulnerability of witnessing ourselves as growing through negative things versus being those things. Vulnerability is the sweet spot where magic truly happens on the journey. Taking empathetic action requires a lot of vulnerability and resiliency, enhanced by the community. Vulnerability can lead to either shame or accountability. As author Don Miguel Ruiz once wrote, "True justice is paying only once for each mistake. True injustice is paying more than once for each mistake." When we stay in shame, we unconsciously commit to injustice, which can lead us to ghost the process.

GHOSTING

Most of us know *ghosting* as a term from the dating world, and we've probably all experienced ghosting to some extent. If you haven't experienced ghosting in your individual relationships, maybe you have in the workplace. It's the feeling of emptiness when it feels like something has just vanished. We've all experienced some form of ghosting on a global scale. For example, we've seen many companies commit to more inclusive workspaces, but not commit to the accountability for it. Some companies even call these efforts part of a five-year plan, which makes it feel like you were gaslit into believing change was possible. That feeling of corporate ghosting is similar to one's personal journey. But when you are the one who has ghosted, the solution is simple. When you know you've moved away, you simply have to recommit to the practice. This is why we say the work requires a relationship, because when shame leads to ghosting, accountability can be held within the community. The way out of ghosting is tied back to self-awareness, learning, accountability, and community.

COMMUNITY

The notion of community is scary for some, especially if you're like me and grew up in evangelical Christianity, which shames you for not falling in line. Now, when I think of community, I don't think of large gatherings of like-minded people assembled for one purpose. I think of two or more folx gathered together with similarities and differences for a larger purpose to connect outside of themselves. The idea isn't that we all have to be, act, and look the same. Nah, that's a cult. My idea of community is acceptance of all those in the space, making space for neurodivergence and actively seeking folx with similar beliefs to work in tandem with you. Community doesn't have to be some monolithic ideology of normalcy (personally, I find that boring). Your community is your soul family, helping you be seen, show you love, and hold you accountable when their interconnected core values cause harm to the collective. A good community embraces agreements for being well, and in the community, you understand there are no disposable people. Your job is to cultivate restoration when harm is caused, as repair is necessary for all to be seen, held, and sustained by the greater collective.

REPAIR

If repair is the umbrella, reparations lives firmly under it. Repair is the process of acting with integrity, aligning your values with the process. You know that repair is necessary because there is no such thing as perfection. You will get this work wrong over and over again, yet you must be willing to own up to your mistakes and admit harm was caused. Note that just because you might offer repair doesn't mean that true restoration can be had. In some cases, many individuals believe that repair means everything is okay. No, this is not always the case. Repair is a process and trust has to be earned over time. Authentic repair requires not having any expectations of the outcome. It requires staying in the messy middle. Most of us want to be likable, but when harm is caused, likability must go out the window. You have to risk being seen as the villain in order to heal forward. This isn't a journey of being liked; it is a call to healing.

YOUR JOURNEY CONTINUES

There isn't a one-size-fits-all approach to this practice; this is a lifelong journey. I can't tell you the destination, I can only encourage you to know that you are on the path forward. You must understand that you *are* born privileged, unconsciously biased and actively complicit in the imperialistic, patriarchal, ableist, and white supremacist systems of oppression. Through practice, sustained effort, and the belief in your own ability to be changed and transformed, you can embody the work. That's the call to this work; the embodiment, the practice, the giving yourself grace to get things wrong is how we heal our way forward and toward liberation.

ACKNOWLEDGMENTS

I would like to acknowledge that this book was written on stolen land in southern Nevada. This land is the traditional land of the Southern Paiute people. I honor the Paiute people who continue to thrive today as the Las Vegas Paiute Tribe and the Moapa Band of Paiute Tribe.

I want to thank my ancestors who came before me. I am because you are.

I want to thank my mother, father, siblings, nieces, and nephews for being a reflection of who I am. I am because you are.

I want to thank Mario, Micah, Melech, and Naima for calling me home to myself at times that I looked outside of myself. I am because you are.

I want to thank Simone and Wes for giving me space to grow into myself. Camden, Jacoby, and Sierra, thank you for being lights in the darkness. I am because you are.

I want to thank the teachers who have crossed over: bell hooks, Desmond Tutu, Audre Lorde, Toni Morrison, Dr. Maya Angelou, Claudette Colvin, Dr. Martin Luther King Jr., Nelson Mandela. I want to thank the elders, the teachers who came before me: Angela

ACKNOWLEDGMENTS

Davis, Oprah Winfrey, Iyanla Vanzant, Dr. Thema Bryant, Rev. angel Kyodo williams, Kimberlé Crenshaw. I am because you are.

I want to thank the future generations who will walk upon the foundation that I am helping to lay. I am because you are.

ReSOURCES AND GUIDANCE FOR CO-CONSPIRɑTORS

"You can tell a lot about a person
by what's on their playlist."
—Begin Again

As I was writing this book I found myself feeling incredibly isolated, stressed out, and overwhelmed. Members in my sacred community reminded me that I could change the way traditional publishing looked by inviting community into my writing process. When I first heard this, I was taken aback. I thought, *How dare you all challenge me this way? I can do this on my own.* But that idea shows how even I struggle with the notion of individualism and wanting to be *the only one.* After being continually called in, I had an "aha" moment, connecting into the African proverb "The load is lighter when two people carry it."

My ancestors were communal. They knew it took a village to help the community thrive. There was never a focus of one, but the synergy of all. After quiet reflection, I knew I could give the idea of community contributions a try. In fact, the *Check Your Privilege* Anthology series was rooted in the idea that our collective stories can speak life into others. If we can write our stories together, other folx can see themselves and move toward their own healing.

Healing isn't linear, which is why the path forward requires a new tool belt to help you keep momentum on this journey. The work isn't a moment; it's a movement, one that requires sustainable support as you work toward reparative healing. In the following pages, I offer tools and resources, such as books, podcasts, and music, to help guide you and regulate your nervous system through the process of unlearning and relearning. Enjoy the tools to support your work ahead. I've split this up into various categories, books for the soul, books to nourish, and books to support your antiracist and decolonization process, and provided feedback from co-conspirators in between the resources. The goal is to read books that support your transformation *and* books to expand your knowledge base. The podcasts recommended are a mix of social justice, life, and healing to bring synergy into your practice. This chapter is a love letter from me and the Check Your Privilege Community offering resources and guidance to inspire you to heal your way forward and toward a reparative future.

What I wish people to know is that my perspective and knowledge on giving co-conspirator guidance is based on the foundations of my lived experience. It takes courage to challenge the White Supremist ideologies of dominance and superiority through systems and structures in your family upbringing. Now that you are ready to unlearn those old systems and are seeking help, directions, and instructions on how you can transition those thought patterns, your life can move forward, allowing you to begin again. Your willingness to become uncomfortable, to face the fears of unknown and unfamiliar belief systems through the interactions of your social inclusion and engagement with BIPOC, is the first step of your journey.

As you begin your co-conspirator journey, visualize and reflect on your upbringing, those systems, behaviors, and values within your family unit and throughout the community existing as shared "Cultural Universals," and for some, the shared religious beliefs where one is valued by kindness and the "Golden Rule," treating others the way you want to be treated, but then only applying that rule to white people. Think about your shared human experience and social engagement. Is it only with white people? Really take a moment and consider how you interact and socially engage with Black people, and how you respond and interact with them.

Here's a work example: A Black employee follows the work process flow for an entire year, audits the process to find conflicting details, and finds out that four wrong individuals were paid. The problem is reported to the supervisor who is white, and the response given to the Black employee is, "I certainly can't guarantee that there won't be lapses in communication in the future, but I will strive and encourage others to be as clear and transparent as possible."

Now in a similar situation with the same account, a different white supervisor replies to a white colleague after similar lapses in communication, "Sorry that this issue wasn't clearly communicated ahead of time." Now both supervisors are nice and kind people, but when you're Black, you cannot give feedback under any circumstances, and if so, it has to be indirect and a proper tone must be used. Can you see how the social engagement is different with the Black person compared to the white person? Can you see the racial bias or racist behavior?

While you are on your journey, here's how I would like to encourage you to unlearn your white supremacy ideologies in a "lived experience way." Okay, now wait, hold on a minute, before I start, I will need to converse with your spirit, your inner soul. That space of "being" within you that is simple and at rest. That "being" within you that suspends judgment and has a willing heart to listen without negative self-talk, that can bask in reflection and pick up on surrounding context clues, learning how to code-interpret. Don't think, just be. Temporarily, be in the moment and practice introversion. Just observe and reflect on what you were taught around the rules of societal engagement and interactions with others, including the good and the bad on topics of racism. Be in that moment, stretch out your arms, palms facing upward, and in the moment of knowing that you are on your journey to becoming antiracist, acknowledge and accept it, say out loud, "I am a racist. My ancestors were racist, and that is who I don't want to be."

Now, subconsciously, your ego is going to do battle with you. It's going to be offended, cause hurt feelings, deny, try not to engage with your thoughts, but silently and forcefully command and demand your ego to "Shut up." Then, speak up in a loud voice, your teacher voice and say, "1, 2, 3, all ears listen carefully. Your affirmation is that I no longer want to unconsciously carry in my Spirit racial prejudice against or toward Black people. Now just inhale 1, 2, 3, and exhale 4, 5, 6. Try not to internalize it, throwing the phrase out of your Spirit, like throwing out the trash. Inhale 1, 2, 3, that is who I no longer want to be, exhale 4, 5, 6.

Now, go on out there and buy books on Black history and critical race theory, continue conversations with Check Your Privilege, and others. I wish you well on your journey, and remember, being "kind" does not equate to accountability. It just means you kind of caused a Black person trauma, and it also means that you're just going to keep being the same old you with a smile on your face. Be better!!

—Susie Hill (a.k.a. my Mom)

SOUL READS

All About Love by bell hooks

Everyday Ubuntu by Mungi Ngomane

Set Boundaries, Find Peace: A Guide to Reclaiming Yourself by Nedra Glover Tawwab

The Altar Within by Juliet Diaz

The Work of Byron Katie by Byron Katie

What Happened to You by Oprah Winfrey and Dr. Bruce Perry

You Were Born for This by Chani Nicholas

In the beginning, most of us tend to devour whatever books we can, learn everything we can in an effort do the "right" things and be the best ally there is in order to be the good white person. The drive is to "fix" things and move on to more comfortable feelings; driven by a mentality based in shame, fear, and pain. But I've come to realize this is a function of white supremacy. Over time, I've seen this path is much less about learning and a whole lot more about un-learning, coming undone and allowing myself to be imperfect, allowing myself to show up in all the ways. In my experience, our bodies are a crucial piece to this. White supremacy has demanded we become dissociated from our bodies, each other, and the Earth.

Our bodies offer a portal back to our natural flow, our power, our intuition, our connection with all that is. It offers us the wisdom needed to re-integrate with the parts of ourselves that capitalism

commodified so we can show up more fully and more authentically. As we lean into the discomfort and learn to hold the space for our collective pain, we come to recognize that there is nowhere to get to, that this is a daily and ongoing practice of unlearning, of inquiry, and of falling apart together. In that connection and co-creation, once you've hung in through the discomfort and messiness, there is this amazing experience of bliss that happens when we fully experience our interconnectedness. We realize there is nothing to fix; the connection has always been there. And from this space we can co-create something entirely different.

—Zoe

Dealing with my addiction to privilege has been some of the hardest and most painful personal work I have ever done. One of my first lessons was that whiteness doesn't see whiteness. The second big lesson was that without dealing with my personal and familial issues around these systems, I was going to continue to do harm. This has required a deep dive into my life's work and relationships. I would never have had the resilience to make changes, to feel in better alignment, if I hadn't been taught that resilience resides in the community and not in the individual.

—Anne M.

It was a harsh awakening when I started my antiracism journey after the death of George Floyd. In the beginning, there was a lot of anxiety, tears, and self-flagellation. I confided in close friends that I *was overwhelmed and embarrassed with how much I did not know or understand. I became a student again. I started reading, watching, learning, following, discussing, and actively listening. But when I took the steps to actively engage in communities outside of my friend circles, the real, magical shift started to happen. The hardest part for me was making that transition—moving from intellectualizing the work to taking concrete action in my community. It was one thing to educate myself with a group of friends and another thing entirely to find my voice out in the real world in a way that could affect change.*

I came to realize the work is not a race, competition, performance, or trend. Being actively antiracist is a lifelong journey. And it is by no means linear. Discover the areas where you are lacking compassion for yourself. Make self-care a practice so you don't ghost the journey and fall into apathy. Let go of perfectionism, which I came to understand is a huge component of white supremacy. Once I realized I was stuck in trying to do it "right," I was able to relax and let the process of becoming actively antiracist unfold organically and naturally. Push through the fear of getting it wrong. Don't be afraid to use your voice. Don't be afraid to amplify the voices of BIPOC. Don't be afraid to be called out and called in. Don't be afraid. You will make mistakes. But I promise you this is soul-changing work. And a soul-changing journey.

—Ellen K.

ANTIRACISM BOOKS

Feminism Is for Everybody by bell hooks

Hood Feminism by Mikki Kendal

How to Be Less Stupid about Race by Dr. Crystal M. Fleming

Post Traumatic Slave Syndrome by Dr. Joy DeGruy

Stamped from the Beginning by Dr. Ibram X Kendi

The Antiracist Business Book by Trudi Lebrón

The Color of Law: A Forgotten History of How Our Government Segregated America by Richard Rothstein

The Fire Next Time by James Baldwin

The Will to Change: Men, Masculinity, and Love by bell hooks

Women, Race and Class by Angela Davis

I wish I had fully understood the concept of "journey." I've come to see that I have a lifetime's worth of conditioning to continually wake up from and unlearn—so this journey is for the rest of my life. It can't be a separate thing I do, it has to be a part of me.

This shift is hard because the layers are endless and there isn't a single thing it doesn't touch—even the expectations I'm conditioned to have about what learning is supposed to look like. It upends your foundation and basic assumptions about yourself and your world. It's disruptive. It affects relationships. It affects everything. So the urge to abandon it, put on blinders, and go back into the warm, cozy cocoon of privilege is strong. It's hard to stay present to not hate yourself, to not drown in shame. I've learned that I need to be accountable for the ways I perpetuate and uphold systems of oppression but also that liberation for all necessitates healing my own wounds.

—Jessica

In my journey, I am still learning and wrestling with the important practice of sensing when to speak less (usually in "safer" situations with people who hold less power and privilege in society) then when to speak up (usually in situations with those who hold more power and privilege and where more is at risk). Until I'm ready to risk my own reputation, my political and relationship capital, I'm probably not ready to truly be an ally.

But first: What are my motivations? Am I trying to make myself look good and aware, or am I vulnerably taking a risk to love, support, and elevate someone else for their benefit? It's about proactively sharing my power, making space for and honoring the contributions of others when they are overlooked or excluded. We can't let the perfect be the enemy of the good or we white people will never say anything—or we say everything, and fill every quiet space with noise that isn't helpful.

Practice and openness to feedback and self-forgiveness become essential. Stepping beyond our comfort zone and speaking truth in the moment for ourselves and for those in our community takes continual practice and a willingness to be vulnerable. We must admit when we're wrong and stay humble and open. It's a deeply spiritual practice of courage, yielding and listening. Patience, patience, patience. May we encourage each other to practice speaking up in smaller situations and teaching our kids the same, so that when the big courageous things present themselves, we've had the chance to build that muscle.

—Eunice G.

My attachment to the identity of "good white person" was the biggest block on my journey—and letting go of it has yielded leaps in my journey. My attachment to this identity produced unhelpful qualities and practices: defensiveness, nervous system flooding and paralysis when presented with accountability or alternative views, righteous anger and dehumanization of others, comparing and feeling "one up" or "one down" from others, disconnection and gaslighting of self and others when presented with the full range of human emotions on the journey, and a lack of compassion for myself and others. Ironically, these behaviors and symptoms are also associated with the symptoms of white supremacy, and they don't work.

What I found was without hyper-vigilance about being a good white person, I freed myself to experiment with relationships and conversations. The results were beyond what I thought were possible. Younger parts of myself grew up, understanding that satisfaction was not in proof of my goodness, but rather in my imperfect action, the humility of accountability, and my growing strength of staying present even in discomfort. I messed up for sure. I was present and accountable. I grew. This created respect for myself and respect from others.

Letting go of attachment to my "goodness" has allowed me to embrace myself as a messy human contributing imperfectly to liberation of myself and others. I believe that our human, vulnerable, and mindful truth-telling and action contribute to dismantling systems of domination. I am grateful to lean into this calling while holding my full range of being: imperfection, falling on my face, celebration of victories, regret and repair, love, anger, action, humility, learning, and impact.

—Sarah L.

PODCASTS

According to Weeze by Louiza Doran

Business Remixed by Trudi Lebrón

Check Your Privilege by myisha t hill

History Shows Us by Lettie Gore

Is My Aura on Straight? by Aycee Brown

Reparations: The Big Payback by Erika Alexander and Whitney Dow

Speaking of Racism by Tina Strawn

The Book Stoop by Row House Publishing, hosted by Amanda Lytle

One thing I wish I had understood earlier is that truthful feedback about how I am showing up can be extremely uncomfortable but that's okay. It's okay for someone to tell me that how I am showing up in this world is causing them harm. This is not a time to put up walls and defend or attack. This is not the time to battle. It's time to listen and understand. It's a time to see this as an invitation to adjust, acknowledge, and set clear expectations of how I choose to move forward with the friendship or relationship. This part of my journey has been the hardest because it calls for me to open myself up to being vulnerable. It means letting go of perfectionism, which is something I used for years to shield myself from being authentic and free. But, while it has been challenging, letting go of perfectionism and opening myself up to feedback lets me have intimate relationships with my friends and family. And yes, there are going to be uncomfortable situations. But there will also be beautiful and authentic moments in my relationships because of this.

—Mitzi

I wish that I had been more aware of how my journey of unpacking my own racism could be harmful or triggering to Black, Indigenous, and people of color. I wish I would have known to be more accepting of my own mistakes and kinder to others for making their own mistakes. I wish I could tell my past self to pray and hold the intention each day to not take things so personally, not to focus on guilt or shame, and to focus more on the journey of taking antiracist actions. I also wish that I had not tried to read every book about racism so fast. It is much more effective to take the time to digest and truly take in information and integrate it. This takes time. Reading and re-reading are very helpful. Listening to audiobooks while walking is also helpful, moving while taking in powerful information helps me retain it. I've learned to listen deeply to each person's experience and become curious about who they are and what their life has been like rather than compare to myself or immediately try to fix or correct anything. Understanding who people are and where they come from and how they've become who they are is important in creating healing communities that can work together to become antiracist. Finding points of connection and common ground, things we can love about each other, and where we need to grow, heal, and educate is very helpful. Immediately canceling people or throw them away without trying to understand where they are coming from leads to a greater divide, but knowing your own capacity to engage and honoring your own boundaries and limits is important too. I think the hardest point for me is when things fall apart when I feel like I've failed and let people down. When I come up against my humanity and my limits, I've learned how to take the time to rest, recover, and find my strength to continue, letting go of whatever it was I was clinging to that led me astray. It's how I've continued to come back to my antiracism journey, understanding the ways that I can make an impact without centering myself or falling into any of the other stereotypical white supremacist ways of "helping."

—Abby K.

One (unexpectedly) significant thing that the co-conspired journey has taught me is the power of and the need for being in community with other co-conspirators. It is a place that supports and encourages vulnerability and the development of deeper self-awareness— all rooted in a solid foundation of accountability. For me, this has resulted in a depth of learning, unpacking, and growth, which is difficult to do in isolation. Bringing full and authentic self to a community felt so contrary to the conditioning and teachings of the systems in which I was raised. But it has been a crucial step in understanding the complexity, and deep nuance of what being a human and thus a co-conspirator, means.

Navigating shame and the complexity of associated emotions and behaviors it elicits has been a very raw, painful part of the journey. But it has also been one of the more profound invitations. I have been invited to develop greater empathy and understanding for others and for self. To better understand that accountability—in holding it for myself and others—is deeply intertwined with empathy. To look beyond and let go of simplifications and binaries. To embrace the whole, beautifully messy human experience. To recognize the harm I have caused/cause (to others and self) and the continuous work needed to not only quit doing so, but to also contribute constructively to change-making. The pain is a very real part of the journey, no one is alone in experiencing it. If I could offer one bit of advice, it would be to strive to engage with it and explore its invitations, leveraging the compassion, support, and accountability of the co-conspirator community to help you do so.

—Whitney S.

ENDNOTES

CHAPTER 1

1. "Can Trauma Be Passed Down from One Generation . . ." Psycom.net. Accessed November 13, 2021. https://www.psycom.net/epigenetics -trauma.
2. "Oppression." Oppression—an overview, ScienceDirect Topics. Accessed November 13, 2021. https://www.sciencedirect.com/topics /social-sciences/oppression.
3. "The Combahee River Collective Statement." Accessed November 13, 2021. https://americanstudies.yale.edu/sites/default/files/files /Keyword%20Coalition_Readings.pdf?ltclid=.

CHAPTER 2

1. Vera Nunning, "Fictions of Empire and the (Un-)making of Imperialist Mentalities: Colonial Discourse and Post-Colonial Criticism Revisited." *Forum for World Literature Studies* 7, no. 2 (2015): 171–198.
2. S. I. Coard and R. M. Sellers, "African American Families as a Context for Racial Socialization," in *Emerging Issues in African-American Family Life: Context, Adaptation & Policy*, eds. V. McLoyd, N. Hill, and K. Dodge (New York: Guilford Press, 2005).
3. Vince Gowmon, "From Caterpillar to Butterfly: Quarantine Is Humanity's Necessary Metamorphic Time in the Chrysalis," Vince Gowmon website, October 3, 2021. https://www.vincegowmon.com /from-caterpillar-to-butterfly/.

CHAPTER 3

1. Michelle Baddeley, "Herding, Social Influences and Behavioural Bias in Scientific Research: Simple Awareness of the Hidden Pressures and Beliefs That Influence Our Thinking Can Help to Preserve Objectivity,"

EMBO Reports 16, no. 8 (August 1, 2015): 902–905, https://doi
.org/10.15252/embr.201540637.

CHAPTER 4

1. In Owen Hargie, *Skilled Interpersonal Interaction: Research, Theory, and Practice* (London: Routledge, 2011).
2. "The Relationships between Listening Preferences, Communication Apprehension, Receiver Apprehension, and Communicator Style," *International Journal of Listening* 17, no. 1 (2003).
3. Americanbar.org. Accessed November 13, 2021. https://www.americanbar
.org/groups/crsj/publications/human_rights_magazine_home
/civil-rights-reimagining-policing/a-lesson-on-critical-race-theory.
4. Mahatma Gandhi, *The Collected Works of Mahatma Gandhi* (India: Publications Division, Ministry of Information and Broadcasting, Government of India, 2000).
5. Martin Luther King, *Stride toward Freedom*, 1958, Papers 5:422.

CHAPTER 5

1. "Education and the Search for Knowledge of Reality: Complete Knowledge, True Knowledge or 'Truth.'" Accessed November 13, 2021. https://www.holisticeducator.com/truth.htm.

CHAPTER 6

1. Juliana Horowitz, Anna Brown Menasce, and Kiana Cox. "Views of Racial Inequality in America." Pew Research Center's Social & Demographic Trends Project. Pew Research Center, September 22, 2021. https://www.pewresearch.org/social-trends/2019/04/09/views
-of-racial-inequality/.

CHAPTER 8

1. bell hooks, *The Will to Change: Men, Masculinity, and Love* (New York: Washington Square Press, 2005).

CHAPTER 9

1. "The Signs of Unhealthy Power Dynamics in a Relationship—and How to Even Them Out." Big Think, September 30, 2021. https://bigthink
.com/neuropsych/power-in-relationships.

ENDNOTES

CHAPTER 10

1. "What Is Abolition, and Why Do We Need It?" Transform Harm, March 1, 2021. https://transformharm.org/what-is-abolition-and-why -do-we-need-it/.
2. Christine Fernando, "Mutual Aid Networks Find Roots in Communities of Color," Associated Press, January 21, 2021. https://apnews.com /article/immigration-coronavirus-pandemic-7b1d14f25ab717c2a29ceaf d40364b6e.
3. "What Is: Indigenous Sovereignty and Tribal Sovereignty," Indigenous Environmental Network, June 17, 2020. https://www.ienearth.org /what-is-indigenous-sovereignty-and-tribal-sovereignty/.

CONCLUSION

1. "Bandwagon Fallacy," Excelsior College OWL, June 6, 2017. https://owl .excelsior.edu/argument-and-critical-thinking/logical-fallacies/logical -fallacies-bandwagon.

ABOUT THE AUTHOR

myisha t hill is a mental health activist, speaker, and entrepreneur passionate about mental wellness and empowerment for all. She runs the advocacy site Check Your Privilege with more than 700K followers on Instagram (@ckyourprivilege). Additionally, myisha works with organizations and community groups taking white and white-identifying people on a self-reflective journey to explore their relationship with power, privilege, and racism.